Some Leaves—
Fallen from Life

SOME LEAVES FALLEN FROM LIFE

Written and Edited by
B. K. KARKRA

RANDOM PUBLICATIONS
(Publishers and Distributors)
NEW DELHI - 110 002 (INDIA)

RANDOM PUBLICATIONS

4376A/4B, Gali Murari Lal, Ansari Road,
Daryaganj, New Delhi - 110 002 (India)
Phone : 011-43580356, 011-23289044
e-mail : sales@randompublications.com
info@randompublications.com
randomexports@gmail.com

SOME LEAVES FALLEN FROM LIFE

First Published, 2014
Reprinted 2018
ISBN 978-93-5111-306-5

Reprint 2021

PRINTED IN INDIA

Published by S.K. Mehra for Random Publications, New Delhi and Digitally Printed at : Replika Press Pvt. Ltd.

Dedicated

The book is dedicated to the memory of my late parents, Sh. B.S. Karkra and Smt. Shanti Karkra, now resting in peace somewhere in their celestial abode.

PREFACE

Presented in the book is a collection of small soulful stories, loaded with some meaning and carrying a subtle message. These have been mostly picked out of my experience of service with the Indian Army, the National Security Guard (better known as the 'Black Cat Commandos) and the Indian Police. Quite a few stories have their origin in what we see around us in life. These are thus in the nature of the leaves fallen from life itself. Besides, there are a few essays to explain the general ethos of various armed forces and police organizations. All these pieces already stand published in various national dailies and some reputed regional newspapers, mostly as 'Middles' on their editorial pages and are being reproduced here with permission/ due attribution.

The 'Middles', placed in the middle of the editorial pages, contain the ethos of an age in germ form. These tend to latch on to the DNA of the times, as these mirror the mind of people and permit us a peep into their soul. These pieces are thus more informative about an age than the raw news floating around. The news fades over a period of time, while the ethos sticks.

The tiny stories in the book are not only the narratives of the situations faced, sensations felt and the difficulties and dangers overcome, but also end up with a punch (surprise element) and delivery of a useful message. These would hopefully tickle the nerves of the reader and make him feel, as if he is reliving some situations of his own life.

The book is in the nature of my sentimental journey through life, particularly my career in the armed forces and police.

B.K.KARKRA

Acknowledgment

The book contains material published in various national and reputed regional newspapers of the country. I am deeply grateful to these newspaper establishments for their kind permission to compile these pieces of mine in book form. I feel particularly indebted to the illustrious cartoonists and photographers for their highly thought-provoking art-work.

CONTENTS

Preface

Acknowledgment

1. LIFE IN THE ARMED FORCES 1

(A) ARMY

Proud of Giving its Today for the Nation's Tomorrow

1. 'Home they Brought her Warrier Dead' 1
2. The First Journey to the Front 5
3. The Army Way of Doing Things! 7
4. A Gentleman Officer 9
5. The Double Check of Gunners 11
6. The Lesson 15
7. The Life Underground 17
8. A'Tandoori' Failure on the Borders 19
9. Soldiers, World Over 21
10. On the Government of India Service 23
11. The Initiation 25
12. The Brave Die Just Once 27
13. The Mysterious Bonds 29
14. London and Monty 31
15. Living by the Sword 33

16. An Institution called Subedar Major 35
17. Izzat-o-iqbal 37
18. The Liaison talents of the Armed Forces 39
19. Superiority Complex 41
20. That Eid of 1857 43

(B) NAVY

The Protectors of the Seas Surrounding us

21. India's Rights in the Surrounding Seas 47
22. Living History 51
23. A Life Check-mated 53

(C) CENTRAL RESERVE POLICE FORCE

The peace-keepers to the nation

24. The High task of keeping the Country together 55
25. The Road through Aksai Chin 61
26. The Martyers who got Short-changed 65
27. Their hour of Agony 67
28. A Great Doer 69
29. A Brush with History at Chikmaglur 71
30. Glow of Warmth 75
31. A Truth Stranger than Fiction 79
32. Hiding History in Eyes 81
33. Duty in Defiance of Tears 83
34. The V.I.P. Rooms at Borjar 85
35. A Soldier Stung Inside 87
36. In the Corridors of Power 89
37. The Return of the Rebels 91
38. A Case of Natural Justice 93

39. The Eternal Cycle 95
40. The Human Face of the Police 97
41. A Thing of Beauty 99
42. An Age Old Illusion 101
43. The first Female Combat unit of the Country 103
44. The Obvious Need for a Third Force 107

(D) NATIONAL SECURITY GUARD

(The Black Cat Commandos)

Designed to Descend on Enemies like a Bolt from the Blue.

45. India's Response to 26/11 111
46. The Monalisa Smile 115

2. THE POLICE ETHOS 117

They produce the precious wealth of peace

47.The Problem of Police image 117
48. Policing the Police 123
49. The Knights in the Shining Armour 125
50. The Difficult Art of Looking Daggers 127

3. THE DAWN OF FREEDOM 129

'Bliss was in that dawn to be alive.......'

51. The Great Surge for Freedom 129
52. The Rise of a Republic 131
53. The Old World Charm 133
54. The Pull of the Past 135
55. A Case of Addiction to Milk 137

4. SOCIAL CONCERNS 139

India, 'with all thy faults, I love thee still'.

56. 'Aam Adami', The Great! 139
57. Conditions apply 141
58. The Stories without an end 143
59. About A Faded Passion 145
60. The Murder of a Morning 147
61. Panic at Palwal 149
62. An Inauguration 151
63. A Valued Client 153
64. Breast-beating for the Poor 155
65. The Age of the Showman 157
66. The three on two Wheels 159
67. A Tale of three Cities 161
68. The Bigger Evil 163
69. The State of the Nation 165
70. A Leaf from an Open Book 167
71. The Cheer Leaders! 169

5. IN THE JAT FRATERNITY 171

Soaked in good natured simplicity and rustic wisdom

72. The Milk of her Kindness 171
73. An Abraisive Tounge, But a Heart of Gold 173

6. LIFE, AS IT IS LIVED 175

Life, a gift that directly descends from God

74. In the Nature of Things 175
75. The Retirement Blues 179

76. Just Next to God 181
77. The Language of Life 183
78. Rising Above Blood 185
79. Nothing to Hide 187
80. In the Queue 189
81. A Brush with the Islamic Laws 191
82. His Majesty—The Common Man 193
83. Wives, World Over 195
84. In Search of Ideas 197
85. Man of the Mountains 199
86. The Great Survivor 201
87. Lines of Loyalty 203
88. The Bicycle Age 205
89. In the Citadel of Islam 207
90. The Human Female 209

7. CURIOSITY 213

The great human urge to know the unknown

91. The Dungeons of Death 213
92. A Close Look at the Gallows 217

8. FROM MY OWN BACKYARD 219

Every story, told in all its intensity, is a 'Booker' candidate

93. In the image of Amir Khusrao 219
94. The Life then 221
95. Fading into Eternity 223
96. Smiling out of Life 225
97. A Short Journey 227

98. 'Apparel oft Proclaims The Man' 229
99. A News for Me 231
100. The Peace-maker 233
101. The Surplus Child 235
102. The Bonds that would not Snap 237
103. A Great Bathroom Singer 239
104. 'Char Bahuraniyan' 241
105. A Mysterious tradition 243
106. A Philosopher in the Family 245
107. The End of a Story? 247
108. Graceful in Grief 249

9. THE THROB OF LIFE 251

Life throbbing, young and quick

109. Baby's Day Out 251
110. The Changing Contours 255
111. Our Budding Innovators 257

1

LIFE IN THE ARMED FORCES

(A) ARMY

Proud of giving its today for the nation's tomorrow.

1. 'HOME THEY BROUGHT HER WARRIER DEAD'

One view is that the nations need 'periodic bleeding' to retain their manhood. The other is that 'a war wastes a nation`s wealth, kills its flower, condemns it to be governed by the adventures and leaves behind puny, deformed and unmanly to breed the next generation'. Perhaps, the truth lies somewhere in between.

Any way, it has never been the concern of a soldier whether a war is good or bad for the country. We, the soldiers, are in the profession of fighting. Our job is to kill on order whoever is declared the enemy of our state. During my time in the Indian Military Academy in the year 1963, the words painted in bold outside our firing range were: 'ONE BULLET, ONE CHINESE'. Obviously, the risk of getting killed in the process is also a part of the game. After all, military victories feed on blood and those who live by the sword have to be ready to die by the sword.

Battle casualties are thus a natural consequence of fighting. If these involve a definite element of tragedy, these also have an unmistakable element of glory in it. In fact, the paths of glory often lead to the graves. These were precisely the thoughts in mind when I joined the Army in the wake of the Chinese aggression on our soil in 1962. All of us were meant to be inducted in the operational areas post haste and were very clear in our minds about our occupational hazards.

Those times were a bit different from now. No one then thought in terms of playing politics while the nation was at war. No political party was prepared to beat its chest over our dying, as some, to our great amusement, did with great gusto during the Kargil war. Possibly, if they had their way, many in the government would be facing prosecution U/S 304A IPC for causing our death by their negligence. We knew that all those who did their duty well deserved to be honoured. So, when we fought well, we expected to be appreciated and nothing more beyond that.

If we became a battle casualty, we had to burn unceremoniously in the battle field itself with generous amount of kerosene sprinkled over us. There was no chanting of mantara's, no burning of incense, no pouring of butter oil (ghee) and no going around our pyres by our sons or brothers. There were times when the cremation parties did not know whom they were cremating. Then there was a bit of improvement in the way of recording the identity of the dead. Those of us posted in the operational areas were required to wear two steel discs, one circular and the other an oval one, all the time. One of these identity discs was supposed to be removed before cremation for record and the other burnt with the body to be the part of the ashes.

To our solace and comfort, all this underwent a sea change during the Kargil war. We then thought of doing with our dead heroes what the Americans had been doing for years. The mangled bodies, riddled with bullets and splinters, were reverently put in nice coffins, neatly draped in the national colours, flown to the airports nearest to their homes and then carried in processions to the grieving relations, bedecked with flowers.

The dead of the earlier wars must be turning in their graves, feeling that the right time to die for the country was now. We, the survivors, see a glow of the martyr's glory within us. I never liked to take sides in politics. Still, I sincerely wished at least a million extra votes to the then ruling dispensation for sending our dead heroes on their last journey well-wept, well-sung and well-honoured.

(A reproduction from the writer's article published in 'The Pioneer' On 20th August, 1990.)

2. THE FIRST JOURNEY TO THE FRONT

I joined the Army in the wake of the Chinese aggression of 1962. I belonged to the very first batch of the Emergency Commissioned officers who had to be rushed to the front cutting short on their training.

I was posted to N.E.F.A. (now Arunachal Pradesh), then a land of mystery to me, for I had earlier never gone beyond Allahabad towards the east. My elder son, Chander Shekhar, was just about fourteen hours old when I had to part company with my wife, Vijay Lakshmi. She still looked in some post-delivery pain and by her side lay a sleepy lump of our flesh, our newborn son.

I had only some vague idea about my place of posting and how exactly to get there. It was drummed into our heads that officers never overstay their leave, unless they are dead. So, I had kept a margin of two days while taking a train to Mokamehghat. The weird journey to my unit headquarters at Lakhimpur then involved two trans-shipments, one by taxi to Barauni and the other to the metre-gauge rail line to Rangia.

By the time I reached Rangia, I found myself among a good number of my batch mates headed for the borders in the North-east. We organized ourselves neatly for the next leg of our journey to Rangapara North. Our luggage was piled daintily right up to the ceiling in the lone first class compartment available with the train. We spread ourselves wherever we could find space like members of a family. It was evening by the time we reached the God forsaken place. The lone train for our next journey was to be available the next morning.

Someone among us had joked that when Tensing Norgay and Sir Edmund Hillary lunged themselves breathless to the summit of Mount Everest, a Sardarji suddenly appeared before them and invited them to his 'dhaba' there. As if to lend credence to this story, a real time Sardarji met us just as our train steamed into the station to whisk us away to his 'dhaba' at the place. Besides, he also owned a bar and a cinema hall. The man gave us a feeling that we were the 'knights in the shining armour' who had come to defend the farthest borders of our country and he was proud to serve and entertain us.

Early next morning, we were on the move again in the train to North Lakhimpur. Most of our people got down at Tezpur on the way and went away waving to us warmly. Seven of us carried on to North Lakhimpur. After reaching the headquarters of our 33 Heavy Mortar Regiment, we found ourselves sitting in the Officers' Mess before our Commanding Officer, Lt Colonel Mackean, son of an Irish father and a Nepalese mother. A fine soul and excellent soldier, he took no time to establish himself as our patriarch. "How many of you are married" he enquired? Three hands went up, including mine. He then asked how many of us had kids. My lone hand went up this time. "Son or daughter and how old" he asked. I said, "Son, sir. Four days old." "What" he said in surprise. I clarified that he was just fourteen hours old when I left home. The grand old man kept it in a corner of his mind.

I was soon on way further to my sub-unit, the 116 Heavy Mortar Battery, then deployed at Ziro in the Subansiri frontier division of N.E.F.A. among the half-naked and heavily tattooed Apatani tribal. After around three months a message came from my regimental headquarters that I would come down to North Lakhimpur. I had not only been sanctioned leave without my applying for it, my kind Colonel had also arranged for my flight in the army courier aircraft to Delhi. Now who would not like to die for the country under such a Commanding Officer?

(A reproduction of the writer's article in 'The Tribune' of 14th September, 2004)

3. THE ARMY WAY OF DOING THINGS!

There is always a right way as well as a wrong way of doing the things. There is, curiously, yet another way: the army way of doing the things. In other words; it means doing simple things in a difficult manner. Those belonging to the soldier's fraternity have probably already understood what I am struggling to say. For the rest, I would like to give an illustration.

We were then the Gentleman Cadets undergoing basic training in the Indian Military Academy at Dehradoon. In the course of our training, we learnt about playing all sorts of wiles and deceptions on the enemy and it was merely incidental that this art came equally handy to hoodwink our own people also.

Sometimes in February, 1963, we, the cadets of the Casino Company were herded into a hall to fill up our bio-data in the dossier forms, sent for the purpose by the Military Secretary's Branch at the Army Headquarters. All of us were handed over a blank dossier form by our Staff Sergeant, one G.S.Bisht, himself a cadet belonging to our senior most batch. The Sergeant had by his side a battery of half a dozen Corporals and Lance Corporals to assist him in the onerous task of getting the forms properly filled by us.

The forms given to us were followed by a thousand words of caution, interspersed with a generous number of threats which briefly meant that if any of us, the blokes, happened to spoil a form all hell would break loose on him.

Against the first serial of the form, we were required to fill up our name in block letters. Half an hour was devoted to tell us how to do it. In fact, the Sergeant himself wrote 'G.S.BISHT' on the black board as a specimen. Still unwilling to take any chances, he invited us to seek clarification for any doubt still lingering in our minds. One overcautious cadet stood up to clarify if he was to fill up Bisht`s name or his own name in his form. This nearly made the Sergeant tear his hair and he barked in anger, "Two hundred front-rolls. Bloody, carry on." The cadet was unceremoniously led out for punishment. Thus, by the time half the form was filled, half of us were doing the front-rolls outside the hall.

By my side sat a hefty Haryanavi, Dharam Singh Shikara and we were now to grapple with a column relating to our educational qualifications. The space provided for the purpose in the dossier form was rather niggardly. Shikara was somehow able to squeeze in his two M.A. and one L.T. degrees there. He did not know what to do with his degree of 'Prabhakar' and the Diploma in Journalism. He was reluctant to seek the Sergeant's help in the matter, as it involved obvious risk. Finally, he came to the conclusion that the Army would not be able to take it all and he brought himself round to just forgetting about his extraneous degrees.

At long last, we came to the end of our ordeal. Now, only our signatures were to be appended. But no, there was no dearth among us of bright fellows asking for trouble. One such character got up to ask whether the signatures were to be in block letters or in running hand. There was a mixed look of anger, amusement and exhaustion on the face of the Sergeant. He would have surely been awarded five hundred front-rolls, if the Sergeant had time on his hands. Fighting the fire inside, he just begged the bloke to oblige him by signing the form in running hand.

Now, this is what is meant by the army way of doing things.

(A reproduction from the writer's article published in the 'Hindustan Times' on 18th November, 1997.

4. A GENTLEMAN OFFICER

The armed forces would always like their officers to have the image of being 'the bravest and the best'. They are expected to do it on the strength of what is known as the officer-like qualities. The phrase O.L.Q. being multi-dimensional in its meaning, it is difficult to draw out its exact contours. When a Babar refuses to get into a cosy cave on an awfully chilly evening and opts instead to sit with his soldiers in the snow outside, and they, on their part, later win for him the battles at Panipat (1526 AD) and Khanua (1527 AD) against heavy odds, one face of the O.L.Q. is beautifully brought in focus.

I had an occasion to see another facet of this phenomenon actually at work while serving at the headquarters of the 2 Mountain Artillery Brigade, located in the North-east sector some 47 years back. I was then a piddling captain with just about three years of service who would instinctively come to attention by the side of the telephone instrument when the brigadier called on it. However, in the absence of a major in our operations branch I had been officiating as the Brigade Major for quite a while. This appointee was then supposed to be the principal staff officer of the brigade.

After a considerable time lag, a substantive major was finally posted to our formation to take over from me. The newly posted officer, Major Kuldip Ludra, liked to project himself as a bully. He lost no time in calling a conference only to tell us how tough he was and what a fabulously rich abusive vocabulary he commanded. I plainly requested him not to try this vocabulary on me at least; otherwise there was going to be trouble for both. Major Ludra must have felt singed in his loins, but he deftly switched over to the next point on the agenda. Nothing much happened on that occasion, but we could see that his hurt ego was bound to explode on us some day.

Our brigadier normally did not come to the Officers' Mess for dinner. So, it used to be the Brigade Major's show there in the evenings. The major was so casual about the whole thing that he did not bother to keep the Mess timings in his mind and almost always came late. One evening, however, he happened to come in time for a change and immediately sent a message for us to report to him in the Mess. I was the first to come and I was still very much in time. But, he thought that I had come late and it was the right opportunity to get even with me. As he opened his oral barrage, I also felt cut up and retaliated by shouting at the Mess waiter to bring a glass of cold water for the Major Sahib. This infuriated him and he demanded my belt in token of my arrest.

However, the officers who followed me also insisted that they were in time. So, wisdom straight away dawned on the major and he returned my belt post haste. Next day when I put up a request to see the brigadier about the incident, he felt a little rattled because he knew that he was bound to face some embarrassment. Still the dignified major did not ask me any questions about it and left for the brigade commander's chamber. After a while, I was also summoned there and I stated all the facts before the brigadier truthfully, including my asking for a glass of cold water for the major.

On his part, Major Ludra gracefully admitted that what I had stated was true and he was sorry for the incident. I was asked to leave thereafter and he was kept back. He looked a little low when he emerged from the chamber, but perked up to his usual self when he saw me. As we exchanged glances, he said, "Yes, yes, I got quite some 'jhar' (rebuke). Shall we now patch up over a glass of beer?" Major Ludra rose in stature in my eyes instantly. He may have been an innocent bully, but he was immensely officer-like.

(Reproduction the writer's article published in the 'Hindustan Times' on 6th February, 1998.)

5. THE DOUBLE CHECK OF GUNNERS

Though the advent of the self-propelled missiles, rockets and now the drones have robbed the guns of some of their earlier importance, the artillery continues to play a crucial role in the battle ground. The infantry and armoured columns often get stranded, if effective artillery support is not available for their manoeuvres. An error on part of the gunners can prove to be extremely expensive both in battle and during training exercises.

For this reason, there is a practice with them to have every order repeated and to exercise double check at every stage. There was a joke floating among us at the time. An artillery officer, who had a tendency to stammer on occasions involving extreme excitement, was on duty at an observation post position to direct gun fire on the enemy during our war against the Chinese. He located a Chinese army column moving towards an already registered artillery target. He passed all orders to the gun position to engage the enemy and just withheld the final order to fire. Every order passed to the guns got repeated, as usual, from the gun position and his wireless operator kept confirming it to him with the words, "Through, Sir". He wanted to order firing when the main body of the column would be right at the target (of course, after keeping in mind the time of flight of the projectiles). However, when it was time to order firing, he got in to a fit of stammering and started struggling with the word, "Fire". As he saw the enemy column disappear from the place into the thick forest nearby, 'the af.. af.. af... af——— on his lips finally ended with 'Fite Moonh' (Get lost, you ugly fellow) instead of 'Fire'. His operator promptly passed, 'Fite Moonh, over'. The gun position duly repeated, 'Fite Moonh, out', in acknowledgement.

The joke apart, we, as the officer-cadets of the Regiment, had an occasion to know firsthand why this extra caution by the gunners is so awfully necessary. The modern guns can effectively engage targets far beyond the visual range. Although the guns have to occasionally resort to direct firing also, most of the time they have to deal with the targets which cannot be seen from the gun position. This indirect fire has to be controlled from a small observation post at some vantage point close to the enemy.

The observation post officer first works out the grid reference of his own position as well as that of the mean position of the target. He also measures the angle of the 'Oscar-Tango' (observer-target) line. All this data is then passed on to the guns for being plotted on the Artillery Board. Thereafter, the ranging process starts to bring the target under accurate fire. The officer at the observation post first asks for one round to be fired. If this round is not on the Oscar-Tango line, a lateral correction is given to bring the round on line. After this the round is brought on the target through the bracketing procedure. For instance, if the round falls short of the target guns are ordered to add 800 hundred yards. If the next round falls ahead of the target, the gun position is asked to drop it by 400 yards. The ranging continues till the target is bracketed within 50 yards. The guns are then ordered to fire a salvo to see if the mean position of impact is right on the target or not. If it is not, another correction is ordered.

Sometimes in May, 1963, we were engaged in such a ranging exercise at the School of Artillery at Deolali. The School has been provided with an adequately large range area for practice firing by the trainees. It has been meticulously mapped and a wide strip on its periphery has been marked as the safety zone. Rest of the area in the middle where rounds can be freely fired is referred to as 'trace'.

We started our maiden firing from an observation post in the range with a great sense of zeal and excitement. Major Kesri Singh, our Instructor Gunnery, was there with us to supervise the firing.

The co-ordinates of our own position were noted on a corner of our laminated maps and we started engaging targets pointed out by our I.G. As the day wore on our initial excitement waned and the whole thing started turning mundane and monotonous. Our I.G. also started feeling a little fatigued. In this state of decreased alert, a cadet who was given a target just outside the 'trace' passed on his own coordinates in place of those of the target to the guns. The safety officer responded from the gun position routinely as per the drill, "Stopped by safety. Round landing out of trace. Safe correction 'ADD 800'." Our I.G. knew that he had selected the target that slightly intruded into the safety zone. He, over-ruling the safety officer, passed the message, "IC——— Major Kesari Singh responsible". The safety officer showed a good presence of mind this time and made the gunners stand fast instantly. He then passed a message to us that the round was landing right on our position. This made many of us, including our I.G., miss a few heart beats. However, all was well in the end. The 'double-check' precaution of the gunners had just saved us from falling prey to our own guns.

(Reproduction of the writer's article published in 'The Pioneer' on of 22nd July,1998)

6. THE LESSON

Our army has a few unwritten golden rules of conduct. One of these, for instance, is 'Never volunteer'. Another is that 'Lieutenants are meant to be seen and not heard'. However, the one I am concerned with here is: 'a senior is always right'. I learnt it quite early in my army career in a little hard way though.

After completion of the 'Y.O.`s (Young officers`) course in the School of Artillery, we, particularly me with distinction in Mathematics in my graduation that is of high relevance to the gunners, had an illusion that we had learnt quite a bit about gunnery and felt what in army parlance is called 'shit-hot'. On completion of my course I had just been posted to 116 Heavy Mortar Battery, along with my course mate, 2nd Lieut. S.K. Gaur. Our battery commander, Major Vazandar, had orders to see that our training was followed up on practical lines in our sub-unit. So, our Major Sahib was ready with his lesson plans transcribed on black boards in different colours. Every subtitle was covered with a paper strip to be uncovered one by one as the lesson proceeded.

Our Battery Commander had no pretensions of being a past master in gunnery. He was well up in his job, though he had gone a little stale with his theoretical knowledge. On the other hand, both of us were a little 'chattack' (over smart) types and being fresh from the School of Artillery, we always managed to cause an embarrassment or two to him almost daily. Whenever we differed with him on some point and the manual was consulted, he was invariably found to be wrong.

Our commander may have been lacking a little in theoretical knowledge, he was not short on tactics. One day when we were at our usual game of making life difficult for him in the class-room, he suddenly switched over to the favourite subject of all seniors— 'hair cut'. His immediate aim was, of course, to ward off our inconvenient queries. Giving us a hard look, he enquired whether we could do him a favour. While we were still trying to guess what he was up to, he thundered, "Have bloody proper hair cut, before you come to the class tomorrow." Now hair cut is an ordeal which everybody has to undergo in the army. I had been given such a merciless first haircut in the Indian Military Academy saloon, despite my persistent urgings, that I wore a near Yul Brynner look for months. By now, however, we were smart enough to make do with a little pruning on the sides to comply with the orders.

Next day the Battery Commander came fully prepared to put us on the mat. After proceeding with our lesson, he suddenly shot, "What is 'droop"?Expectedly, there was a look of confusion in our eyes and a glimmer of victory in his. He was, however, not finished yet. To consolidate his victory, he bombarded us with the next question, "What is yaw"? Both of us were again nonplussed and looked lost. Next half an hour was duly devoted to give us a thorough dressing down for the pathetic state of our professional knowledge. It was only after we had thus been sufficiently softened to his satisfaction that he bothered to explain to us the meaning of these terms. 'Droop' means the angle between the axis of bore of a gun and the line joining the centres of the barrel at the breach and the muzzle end— it points to a defect in the barrel. 'Yaw' is the angle between the tangent to the trajectory of a shell/bomb and its axis which is indicative of a defect in the ammunition. These words had been picked up for our benefit from the précis of the Long Gunnery Staff Course of the School (an advanced training programme for much senior officers) and were of little relevance at our basic level.

Nonetheless, the last laugh went to our commander who taught us yet another important lesson, "Never act smart with your seniors."Anyway, after thus securing our unconditional surrender, the Major Sahib was very kind to us during the rest of our training with him.

(A reproduction from the writer's article that appeared in the 'Hindustan Times' on 7th Sep., 1998.)

7. THE LIFE UNDERGROUND

We have known life without electricity at our home. We have even spent a few months in the late 1940's without kerosene and had to make do with costly candles. We were just on the brink of switching over to the good old mustard oil earthen lamps when kerosene supplies mercifully got restored.

Similarly, when I got posted to my 116 Heavy Mortar Battery in N.E.F.A (now Arunachal Pradesh) in 1963, we found ourselves requesting our army divisional commander, Major General J.S. Aurora, to kindly allow us to live over-ground in tents. The general, however, felt that we were increasingly getting soft. He insisted that we were deployed against the Chinese in an operational area and must get used to living underground in bunkers.

We knew what it meant living in the damp and dingy interiors, with three layers of ballies (wooden logs) and a few tons of mother-earth over us. Despite there being some P.V.C. sheets spread over the roof of the bunker, rainwater always managed to seep inside. When it rained heavily, droplets of water fell all over to make life all the more miserable for us. Mice, cobras, kraits, pit-vipers and the like had free access to our make-shift roof and made their presence quite felt. The only little protection against these, while we slept, was our mosquito-net. So, inwardly, we felt that the general had no idea about our discomforts, as he himself was living in the luxury of a bamboo basha (hutment) at his headquarters.

My 116 Heavy Mortar Battery was then placed in direct support of an infantry battalion, the ¼ Gorkha Rifles, commanded by Lt. Col. Sethi, a fine soldier. The colonel was equally unhappy that our divisional commander was unmindful of our woes. Fortunately, when the general came for his annual inspection it was raining heavily. He insisted on going to the battalion commanders' office and our colonel was happy to take him there. The office, also in a bunker, was under two feet of water that had seeped in. The table top was just about six inches above the water level. In fact, a few sheets of paper were floating around.

The general was too shrewd not to understand what we were trying to convey. He had an amused look on his face. He knew that the Chinese were quite a few days march from our location and really believed that his command must not suffer the discomforts not really written in their destiny. So, he relented and let us leave our damp bunkers to live over-ground in tents.

On his part, Col Sethi assured him that we would keep our bunkers in good state of maintenance and remain in readiness to rush underground at a moment's notice.

We felt deeply indebted to our general for being sensitive to our needs. This general, as the G.OC-in-C of the army eastern command, was to later to preside over one of the finest moments of our history—the surrender of the East Pakistan army before him at Dhaka in 1971.

(A reproduction from the writer's article in 'The Times of India' of 19th November, 2001.)

8. A 'TANDOORI' FAILURE ON THE BORDERS

The one who said that armies march on their stomach was not wide off the mark. The cooks in the armed forces, thus, play their humble role in keeping their units fighting fit. Army cooks are the most hardworking people. They are the first to get up in the morning and the last to go to sleep. Their emoluments and the job profile being low, our army cannot hope to secure proper chefs for their messes. They have to mostly do with the raw hands in the profession who are inducted in the force after a short stint of training.

One such simple soul landed in our unit deployed in Arunachal Pradesh. The man carried the rank of a Special Cook and drew a fabulous extra salary of five rupees per month over and above that of the other cooks of the unit. He was a high-spirited fine fellow, but there was one problem: he did not know how to cook.

There was, however, no option with us but to accommodate him as our head cook in the officers' mess. We were located close to Digboi in Assam. The place had a nice Chinese restaurant which we visited quite often for a change. Lest we should end up eating frogs' legs and some other such delicacies (which though agreeable to the taste buds, could otherwise be distasteful to us psychologically) we always took care to order safe dishes like chowmein, chopsuey and chicken or prawn fried rice.

Our head-cook did not at all relish the idea of his 'saab lok' having to go to a restaurant while he was around. One day I found him furiously fabricating something that looked like a 'tandoor'. He proudly proclaimed that we would soon forget our way to the Digboi restaurant, as he was going to serve us all sorts of 'tandoori' delicacies in our own mess. I, as the Mess Secretary, knew only too well what was waiting to befall us. Yet, I did not want to hurt his feelings. The next day he offered to prepare tandoori chicken for us. Everyone was excited over the prospect of having at least the humble 'Kake-da-dhaba', if not a Moti Mahal coming up at our God forsaken place.

The local A.S.C. officer was sweet-talked in to providing around a dozen small chicks to us. These were put at the disposal of our head cook. The fellow was seen working on these all day. Our longest day was ultimately over as we moved to the dining hall after a few customary drinks. First came the soup and then the much awaited tandoori chicken. My heart missed a beat as the chicks on our plates had look of the Egyptian mummies. Sure enough, nobody could cut a piece out of these to put in mouth. When it became evident that the chicks would start flying around, if any more pressure was applied on them with forks and knives, all of us gave in. Instead we took an odd piece of bread with butter and a few finger chips and got up on near empty stomachs.

We then retired quietly to our rooms, as complaining there and then about the food would have amounted to bad manners. After a while, of course, our officers could be heard shouting to their orderlies to bring them six-egg omelettes from the mess. When I was up on my feet the next morning, I noticed that our much cherished 'tandoor' had already been dismantled and our head-cook bore a look, as if he would break in to tears at any time. I finally managed to console him by offering him another go at us sometimes soon.

(A reproduction from the writer's article in the 'Hindustan Times' of 3rd April, 2003.)

9. SOLDIERS, WORLD OVER

They are in the profession of killing all right, but this, in their case, is considered honourable. The soldiers kill to order just anybody who is declared as the enemy of their state. Once our brigadier asked us during a seminar as to what our weapons were meant for. I cautiously replied that these were meant to neutralize the enemy and to break his will to fight. He thundered, "Our weapons are bloody meant to kill the enemy". This left me wondering how we are then different from the 'supari killers', especially when the states that we may happen to be serving are themselves roguish— take, for instance, the cases of Nazi Germany, Saddam`s invasion of Kuwait or the recent American action in Iraq.

My own experiences in the profession were to later set all these doubts at complete rest. I retired as a soldier some 24 years back, but I often feel that I am still in it— after all, once a soldier, always a soldier. Additionally, I had the privilege of putting on three different uniforms in my career in the armed forces—the olive-green of the Army, khaki of the C.R.P. Force and black/grey of the National Security Guards (better known as the Black Cat commandos).

I have, however, ended up believing that colour really does not matter in case of a soldier. They are not only above the colour of the uniform, but also the considerations of caste, creed and countries. That is how when a Lt General Niazi, after surrender of the Pakistan forces at Dhaka in 1971, asks his senior brother soldier as to how well he fought him, he is candidly told by a Lt General J.S Aurora that in his (Niazi's) circumstances, he himself would not have done any better. You rarely get such gracious answers outside the fraternity of the soldiers.

Years after my retirement, I had another occasion to go to Srinagar as make-shift director to shoot some segments of a documentary on the C.R.P. Force. The sight of my boys in their operational gear sent a flutter through my heart. It was a pleasure to be moving among them again.

After finishing with our shooting late in the evening, we were invited for dinner by our Inspector General of Police, D.D. Gupta, another fine soldier. He was then in operational command of all the C.R.P.F. units in the state of Jammu and Kashmir. When we were enjoying our drink, the I.G.P. commanding the Special Operations Group of the local police dropped in and it was decided to visit our outposts in the city by night.

The armed forces' conveys then often got sprayed with the militant bullets. Our I.G.P., therefore, took care to put the S.O.G. commander in the middle of the back seat that is considered to be comparatively the safest position in the event of the car coming under a hail of bullets. He himself sat by his side and asked me to sit on his other flank. After all, the local police officer was our guest. As for me, a former officer of the Force, he thought that soldiers never retire. It was heart-warming to note that he chose to deal with me, as if I was still in service. On the way, the militants did fire on us indiscriminately from some distant hideout, but their bullets missed us by metres.

(A reproduction from the writer's article in 'The Tribune' of 13th June, 2005.)

10. ON THE GOVERNMENT OF INDIA SERVICE

Babur, the founder of the Mughal empire in our country half a millennium back, wrote in his 'Babur Nama' that only things good about 'Hindustan' were that it was a big country and it had plenty of gold. Otherwise it was 'a country of few charms'. In line with this, what one could safely say today is that the only thing good about the Indian government is that it is a source of livelihood for a vast number of people. In addition, one could also take pride in the fact that this is the only place where donkeys, horses and race-horses were treated alike in our high traditions of a socialistic society. The servile duffers, rather than the real bright ones, stand better chance of prospering here. Otherwise, one must have the extra-ordinary brilliance of a Shreedharan, a Kurian, a Swaminathan or a Petroda and the like to get noticed.

I was then an army captain posted as a personal staff officer to a brigadier who commanded four artillery regiments. One of the regimental commanders felt, at one point of time that he had already worked quite hard and was due for some rest. When he complained of persistent headaches, he automatically became a case of check up for brain tumour in our Base Hospital and consequently, due for a prolonged rest there.

My brigadier always wanted me to keep a track on his treatment. Even now, I am not sure whether he was really anxious about his medical condition or just wanted to catch hold of him for malingering. Perhaps, it had something to do with both. Anyway, once he asked me about the colonel's condition, I innocently explained that an x-ray was taken of his skull and nothing was found inside. I was immediately up for a high jump for missing on the word 'abnormal' in hurry, but the colonel also did not prosper greatly. Unfortunately for many, the armed forces is one wretched place where donkeys and horses get segregated fairly soon.

Now, a sample from the civilian world also, bursting at the seams. The British left our country well over half a century back, but the hangover of their days is still very much there. Even now, the paid servants of the people see themselves to be on the side of the rulers and the citizens as their subjects. They pass good part of their office time playing cards, gossiping, patronizing the tea stalls and 'chaat' venders or knitting at their seats.

They cannot be blamed because often there is nothing more useful for them to do in their offices. This, our friend from the Indian Police, had, however, been able to find a better solution to the problem of killing time. He managed to get himself suspended from service and utilized the opportunity to study for his doctorate. Whenever he met his colleagues, he devoted considerable time to explain to them the advantages of being under suspension. Had his advice been taken, many of them would have missed being the director's general of police. It is not clear though whether they would have otherwise ended up higher on the happiness index.

Nonetheless, when another high profile friend of mine was in a 'To be, or not to be' state of mind while facing a violent mob, his genius gave him a rather simple Bacon-like advice: If in a situation your mind is absent, so should be your body. The valuable advice was again not taken, but I still often feel puzzled whether it was not at least worth a look.

(A reproduction from the writer's article in the 'The Tribune' of 30th December, 2003.)

11. THE INITIATION

At the time of my commission in the army, my wife was in an advanced stage of pregnancy. So my first choice was for posting to a peace station to begin with. Next to that was an assignment in the Jammu and Kashmir sector which lies close to Punjab, my home state. The posting to the North-east was the last thing on my mind.

Nonetheless, as luck would have it, I got posted to the 33 Heavy Mortar Regiment which,at the time, happened to be located in Arunachal Pradesh (then known as N.E.F.A.). My first reaction, quite obviously, was that of a little disappointment. However, when I actually landed at the place I felt strangely rejuvenated by its natural beauty. What rang in instantly my mindwere the lines from a famous lyric which I remembered as, " Yeh nazare, yeh hawa, yeh chandini, jee mein aata hai yahien mar jaeyeeh (The landscape, the breeze and the moon-light are all calling upon me to end up here itself). In fact, that was what we had come here for—to be ready to die for the country, with a thought on our mind: 'Kande wargi jawani kee maen phookni aye, baith gaye jadon bhoond gulab uttey' (Of what use is our strapping youth, if we allow the enemy to violate our motherland).

I had never tasted liquor before reporting for duty here. But, now I knew it was going to be a long haul for me in the solitude of these hills, with the olive-green colour and the semi-naked 'Apatani' tribal for company. So, I took a conscious decision to initiate myself in to drinking.

It was our 'dining –in' night in the officers` mess of the ¼ Gorkha Rifles to which our 116 Heavy Mortar Battery was attached for direct support. Lt Col Sethi, the commanding officer and Major Gurung, the Second-in-command of the unit inspired both love and respect. We, the new officers, four in number, were lavishly looked after with drinks. Only I somehow quietly managed to remain guarded through all this.Finally, when all the four of us were thought to be ready for fun, we were told that it was customary to pull the new officers through the barrel of an artillery gun. Despite, the drink in our stomachs, the prospect made us quite jittery— our guns were barely of 4.2 inch calibre. To our relief, Captain Ahluwalia, the adjutant, announced after a while that the C.O. had instead decided to pass us through the chairs.

I saw my three ebullient friends getting entangled under the chairs to the amusement of the gathering and but finally extricating themselves triumphantly. When it was my turn, I offered to do the same, if that was what my C.O. desired, but I was otherwise all right. The C.O. immediately reacted, "Ab bhi hosh ki baten karta hai, ise aek 'thullo' (a large peg in gurkhali) aur pilao". (He is still talking sense. Give him another large peg). Another 'thullo' in, it was instantly brought home to me why people after all drank. All now seemed to be well with the world and it seemed to be full of friends.

Over the next few years, I also learnt that it was terribly important to remain in moderation over the drinks, otherwise instead you stood every chance of getting consumed.

(A reproduction from the writer's article in 'The Tribune' on 29th January, 2007.)

12. THE BRAVE DIE JUST ONCE

The brave die only once and the cowards die a thousand deaths in their lives before the final one. This is the conviction that our Army carries and this is what I learnt when the premature burst of a faulty mortar bomb fired by us during the course of our training in 1963 sniffed life out of our high profile trainer, a Subedar and left many of us writhing in pain, having been hit by its splinters.

I belonged to the very first batch of the Emergency Commissioned Officers recruited in the wake of the Chinese aggression on our soil in 1962. The war had taken quite a toll of our young officers and the setback to our armed prowess had given some wrong ideas to the Pakistan Army also. They started thinking that we were the pushovers and could be easily dislodged from Kashmir. We were thus desperately needed on the borders. So our training was rushed through. After just three months training in the Indian Military Academy at Dehradoon, I was assigned to the Regiment of Artillery and sent for specialized training to the School of Artillery at Deolali.

After a stint of basic training on our good old 25 pounder field guns, we were allotted our branches. I thus became a mortar gunner. A mortar is a simple smooth barrel gun. Since its barrel is not spirally grooved like that of the other guns and howitzers, a bomb does not have to rub hard against inner walls of the barrel on being fired. As a result, the mortar bombs, as against the artillery shells, have much thinner capsules and can thus be stuffed with much more explosive material. On exploding, the mortar bombs get fragmented in to much larger number of splinters that can wreak havoc on the infantry exposed in the open.

I, being a first class graduate, with distinction in mathematics, had a preference for more sophisticated guns. But my slight disappointment on this score was soon overcome when I learnt that it was the mentally and physically tougher gunners who were assigned to the mortar regiments. After all, the mortars have the maximum mobility. If needed these could even be carried to the Mount Everest, where even the mountain guns cannot go.

By the way, an Everest expedition had once toyed with the idea of firing oxygen cylinders to the South Col of the Everest to save on time and effort. The idea was abandoned because the cylinders could get sprayed over a large area, making their recovery a hard task and also, the firing of mortars could unleash big avalanches in the region.

Coming now back to the practice shooting of the mortars by us, the deceased J.CO. was cremated with full military honours and the injured received prompt attention in our hospital. The very next day, we were taken to the same spot where the ghastly accident had occurred and the firing exercise was resumed. We fired our guns with great gusto, determined in our mind that we will die if God so willed, but just one death.

(A reproduction from the writer's article in 'The Tribune' of 8th August, 2007.)

13. THE MYSTERIOUS BONDS

The officers of the armed forces are in a very unworldly sort of relationship with their men. The exact contours of this bond are impossible to explain. Often it appears that there is a distance of light years between them. Then, suddenly you find that they are the closest kin.

With their bombs and vehicles, the artillery units of the army are rather bulky outfits. Our 33 heavy Mortar Regiment, thus, maintained a big rear headquarters in the plains of Assam whereas its tactical headquarters was up in the Himalayas deployed against the Chinese. I was placed in command of the elements in the rear as a young captain. My logistic subunit was a sort of gateway to the regiment, with the personnel, stores, equipment and vehicles moving up and down all the time.

Frankly speaking, nobody really likes the seniors breathing down his neck. They are welcome only in the crises situations when their guidance is critically needed to show the way and to hold the hand. I, therefore, tremendously enjoyed my little independent command so early in my career. This was, however, too good to last forever. As the condition of roads in our area of operation improved, it was decided to wind up our rear establishment and to merge it in the main body of the unit.

Our move involved crossing the mighty Brahmaputra from Dibrugarh to Sonarighat in the civilian ferries that catered to civilian movements also. We had to do nearly fifty trips in these ferries at the height of monsoons. A return trip at the time involved nearly nine hours. I had to once do two trips in a day to supervise the move of our elements. I felt quite tired and weary. How I wished that I could get to my camp quickly and retire to my bed after a few drinks in comfort. However, we had miles to go as we were in the middle of the river which looked like sea.

I do not know how my men read my need. They produced a bottle of rum from nowhere and poured around three ounces in a mug and held it rather affectionately before me. When I asked them to get some water, they mischievously said that they had no water with them. They even had the audacity to enquire whether they could get me some from the river. I threw a look at the thick yellow liquid flowing noisily to our sides and gulped the rum neat like a dose of bitter medicine. When they saw me grimacing, they readily produced a bottle full of water with their tongues tucked in cheeks. So, the rogues had played a prank on me— the one who they seemingly held in so much awe.

Never mind, the lengthening shadows of the evening, the fast flowing current and a few ounces of rum taken on empty stomach soon wove their magic and I got lost in whirlwind of ideas. It did not take much time for me to realize that what appeared to be quite some distance between me and my men was, in fact, just a thin exigency of command. Otherwise, we were so close to each other in reality.

(A reproduction from the writer's article in 'The Tribune' of 15th April, 2009.)

14. LONDON AND MONTY

I joined our Army more than a decade after the British had left our shores. We, however, still felt their presence in the Indian Military Academy, Dehradun. The remnants of the Anglo-Saxon culture still permeated our routine. Quite a few things were good about the British ethos which we could gainfully retain. Some memories of their time, however, needed to be thrown out of the nearest window. Their apolitical and professional approach to the military career was worth emulating. Their theory in the Indian context that the officers were the individuals and the men only a mass, deserved to be given a hasty burial. It needed to be inculcated that all of us were just human.

The armed forces commanders at all levels find themselves in a unique predicament. At least within their own command, they must radiate the image of being 'the bravest and the best' all the time. They can be friendly and patronizing, but cannot afford to be chummy with anybody, not even with their seconds-in-command. They often feel what is described as the loneliness of command— the tops, after all, are the lonely places. They just cannot open their heart to anybody in their units and formations.

Yet, some of them are highly communicative when it comes to narrating their private experiences in service, particularly in battles. We had our Brigadier Prakash Nath posted out. He was a tough taskmaster and it was by no means an easy job to be his staff officers. Still we were not that uneasy working with him, as he was very true to himself and a genuine person, though not a very amiable one. We were rather apprehensive what his successor would be like. Whether he would like to ask for dinner too early to deprive us of our evening fun in the officers' mess or he would make us sit in the mess well past midnight and then expect us to be up on our feet for the morning P.T.

We finally landed with Brigadier Bikram Chand, a simple-minded soldier. All was well with him, except for the fact that he happened to serve under Monty (Field Marshall Montgomery) and also do a short course of training in London. So, when we met in the mess every evening, we found him too full with Monty and London. We had to go mentally prepared to listen to his repeats on these two subjects that often began with, "You see, where Monty went wrong….." and "You see, when I was in London….".

I was once obstinate enough to ask him what he was when he served under Monty.

Refusing to take the hint that I was taking a dig at his finding fault with the strategies of the legendary field marshal, he innocently replied that he was a second lieutenant then. Similarly, we did not like to be served the staple diet of his experiences in London on daily basis. There was, however, no remedy for all this, except to escape to the toilet too frequently to shake L and M (London and Monty) from our system for a while.

(A reproduction from the writer's article in 'The Tribune' of 24th March, 2010.)

15. LIVING BY THE SWORD

'Those who live by the sword, die by the sword". The words come from none other than Jesus Christ and were spoken in the context of the Zealots, engaged in an underground rebellion against the Roman occupation of Israel two millennia back. Like the terrorists of today, they were not only inviting Roman reprisals on themselves but also on their compatriots. Jesus did not at all like the idea of their half-baked armed struggle. Thus, what he meant was that since the Zealots had chosen the path of violence, they should be prepared for violent reprisals also.

Nonetheless, these words have a positive connotation also and apply equally to the soldiers engaged in the profession of fighting. Since they live by the sword, some of them have to die by the sword. All of them may not get involved in wars in their career spans. Yet, they have to face border skirmishes, deal with terrorists and trouble makers of all hues, operate in tricky terrains and engage in war games and other risky manoeuvres. Most of the times, they would have mines, mortar bombs, grenades and the like for company. However, it is the very defiance of death that gives the soldiers their sense of elan.

While serving in the armed forces, I actively participated in wars, insurgencies, anti-terrorist operations and armed skirmishes. However, it was during peace that I came close to losing my life on a number of occasions. Once during the course of a shooting practice by my heavy mortar battery, some bombs went blind i.e. these did not explode on percussion with the ground. One of my gunners picked up such a bomb, the fuse of which had got detached as a result of the concussion of firing. The bomb without fuse was safe to handle, but the gunner made the mistake of picking up the fuse also which is a sort of mini bomb. The fuse being armed exploded with a slight application of pressure and he had his hand blasted. Had the fuse exploded while fitted in the bomb, all of us around would have been blown to smithereens.

Twice during the grenade firing exercises, we barely escaped getting perforated. In one curious case, the grenade barely managed to get boiled out of the discharger cup of a G.F. rifle and then fell back into it after casting its safety clip. It was thus ready to explode in the cup after seven seconds. Showing an admirable presence of mind, the firer threw the rifle away in time for us around to escape unhurt.

The most bizarre incident of my life, however, occurred when a primed grenade was put in the hand of a rooky trooper to throw. The fellow lost nerve and placed the grenade on the butt saying, "Sab, yeh mere bus ka rog nahin hai" (Sir, it is beyond me). More than four seconds passed in taking notice of the simmering grenade and reacting to the situation. It was swept away by company commander Sandhu just in nick of time, with a big abuse for defaulter. Instantly, we fell breathless over one another in the trench. The grenade exploded a split second later and the sand bags placed on the butt got filled with its splinters. We, the soldiers, however lived to fight yet another day.

(A reproduction from the writer's article in 'The Tribune' of 3rd November, 2011)

16. AN INSTITUTION CALLED SUBEDAR MAJOR

IT is difficult to describe the position and prestige that a Subedar Major enjoys in a unit. Whatever you say about him would fall short of the parameters of his personality. He is rather an institution in himself. His commanding officer often falls back on his advice in difficult situations—specially, those related to the morale, welfare and discipline of his men and the image of the unit. Most of the clout that he commands comes out of the position of trust that he enjoys with his commanding officer who regards him as a repository of wisdom, sagacity, sobriety, maturity, loyalty, cool-headedness and above all, a sort of farmer's horse-sense. But, this is not all. Let me try to explain this phenomenon more properly through a couple of incidents.

An army unit was on an operational exercise in a highly undulated and slippery area. Their divisional commander, a Major General, came to oversee them. When being escorted to the exercise area, he slipped and fell on the ground.Seeing the plight of the embarrassed General, the Subedar Major of the unit, following behind his C.O., lost no time in slipping himself in an equally ungainly thud. He then stood up smartly and said, "Saab, yahan to hum roz bees bees bar girte hain (Sir, we fall here scores of times every day)". That put the General at ease instantly, though he did not fail to notice, rather approvingly, why the Subedar Major had enacted all this. Here was a typical Subedar Major discharging one of his multi-dimensional roles to perfection.

Some 32 years back, the 51 Battalion, C.R.P. Force that I commanded was doing training under an Army brigade at the peak of summer. Our men then did not get any ration allowance. So, their messing had to be managed within their own meagre resources. Something affordable was needed to be done to save them from heat stroke. I directed that they would be served daily two glasses of diluted milk beverage (lassi). Almond, rose and other essences were to be added for flavour. This worked well, in that none of my men was laid with heat stroke and they enjoyed the drink also. . Encouraged with this, I got another brain wave. The summer was now over. I briefed my faithful Subedor Major Sahib that the sub-units would prepare 'kanji', a black carrot based beverage that also works out cheap and is quite tasty and invigorating. Thus, massive 'matkas' (earthen pots) were promptly procured in the unit to brew the beverage for the men. After a few days I checked with my Subedar Major how the idea had done with the men. With his usual sense of obedience, he stated that they were duly being made to drink it 'hukamiya' i.e. under orders. On my prodding, he came out that otherwise the men did not like it. The incident explains yet another facet of a Subedar Major's profile. There are, of course, countless others to it too.

(A reproduction from the writer's article in 'The Tribune' of 4.1.2010)

17. IZZAT-O-IQBAL

Some two hundred years back, the military genius of Napoleon discovered that the primary role of artillery was to provide covering fire in support of the infantry manoeuvres. Earlier armies world over thought that guns were just meant to soften the enemy positions by preparatory bombardment or to hold the attackers at bay through defensive fire.

'Izzat-o-Iqbal' is the motto of the Regiment of Artillery of our own army. 'Izzat' (honour) and 'Iqbal' (prestige) of the gunners lies in their ability to land shells wherever, whenever and in whatever quantity required by the Infantry, 'The Queen of the Battlefield'.

On completion of my basic training in gunnery, way back in June, 1963, I was posted to the 116 Heavy Mortar Battery, then deployed in support of I/4 Gorkha Rifles battalion in the Subansiri frontier division of N.E.F.A. Within a couple of months of my joining, it was time for my battery to undergo the annual course-shooting. During this practice firing, both tactical as well as technical skills of the gunners are to put to a sort of acid test.

The modern guns are capable of projecting shells to distances well over twenty-five kilometers. It is, thus, normally not possible to see from the gun position where exactly the rounds are landing. The fire has to be, therefore, directed from a small O.P. (observation post) overlooking the enemy positions. The coordinates of the O.P. and the Oscar Tango (observer-target) line are passed on to the gun position and these are marked on the artillery board. All the corrections to bring fire on the target are given in relation to the O.T. First, the round is brought to this line and then the target is bracketed within 50 yards through a process called ranging.

The Commander Artillery of our brigade, Brig. Surat Singh, sat with us at our O.P. position to oversee our firing. While all of us waited tensely, he pointed out a target in the range area for me to engage. I briskly moved to the O.P. bunker trying to look cool and confident. Even when I realized that I had forgotten to take my prismatic compass with me to measure the angle of the O.T., I did not panic. Going back would have certainly meant delay and adverse notice.Fortunately, I was familiar with various features in the area and could guess the bearing of the O.T. fairly accurately. The guns were given the orders in the set sequence. One of the guns boomed to my order, but the round was lost in the thickly forested terrain.

But thanks to an open patch of land close to my target, I found an answer to my problem. I asked for a fresh round in the centre of this patch. To my great relief, the burst of this round was clearly seen. The fire was then shifted on to the target through a series of corrections. As the last round landed within the fifty yard bracket, I ordered all guns of the battery to fire a salvo.The M.P.I. (mean point of impact) of the rounds being right on the target, I was now ready to punish it.

The Commander Artillery, however, stopped me from ordering further firing to conserve ammunition and called me up to give his comments on my shooting prowess. He was a man of few words. As I stood to attention to hear his verdict with baited breath, he declared that it was a good shoot, confidently taken. He further said that had there been any enemy at the target, I would have blasted the bastard. The Brigadier's words were music to my ears. These meant that both my 'Izzat and Iqbal' were to be secure, at least through the course of the next one year.

(A reproduction from the writer's article in 'The Hindustan Times' of 9.7.1998.)

18. THE LIAISON TALENTS OF THE ARMED FORCES

The liaison men of the armed forces are certainly a breed apart. One of them was this Naib Subedar Kanwar Singh of my 33 Heavy Mortar Regiment. Way back in 1962, a Battery Commander of the unit, one Major O.P. Khosla, had failed to take timely delivery of his bicycle at the Guwahati railway station. Over the period, the demurrage on the bike had swollen close to the value of the vehicle. So, he instinctively remembered our liaison specialist, Kanwar Singh. His brief was to recover the major's bike without paying any demurrage.

Next day, the major and his wife saw him from a distance talking to the parcel officials, with grief writ large on his face. Soon he had been offered a chair and a cup of tea. For nearly an hour the parcel clerks were seen running here and there to consult their seniors. After a while, Kanwar Singh was walking towards the waiting couple with their bike. The secret behind this exploit was out years later when Kanwar Singh, after consuming a few large pegs of rum, confided in me that he had told the railway men that Major Khosla had gone missing after the 1962 operations and was possibly a battle casualty. This had melted them enough to find ways and means of releasing the bike without demurrage as a special case.

Another brilliant liaison talent was my friend, Vohra, then posted at the C.R.P. Force headquarters. His boss, somehow, thought that Vohra had all the time in the world to sort out his multifarious personal problems. This time, he wanted him to arrange for his child's admission to a sought after public school. Next day, Vohra was before the school principal exercising the cultivated charm of a liaison officer on the lady. She was half-impressed and half-amused over his sweet talking, but was ultimately unable to help.

An ordinary mortal would have straight away told his boss that admission was just not possible and earned his wrath. Wise man Vohra, however, suggested to his senior to accompany him to the principal. He assured him that his sheer personality impact would clinch the issue. When the elated man appeared before the principal along with Vohra, the exasperated lady simply refused to listen to him and in fact, tore into him with some sarcastic words.Particularly stinging was her remark that he did not seem to understand anything, though he claimed to be a senior officer.

All the way back, it was Vohra's turn to do the talking. His liaison skills were now needed to lift the deflated man's spirit and convince him that an institution with, such a swollen head at the helm, was hardly suitable for his child.

(A reproduction from the writer's article in 'The Times of India' on 16.8.2002.)

19. SUPERIORITY COMPLEX

I have been a rolling stone all my life and have, thus, seen life from many angles. Of particular significance is my encounter with both the civil and military ethos. I have served in the regular army, paramilitary forces such as the central Reserve Police Force, Territorial Army, National Security Guard and even in some purely civilian organizations like the Bhakra Nangal Project and the income-tax department etc. I, therefore, have a fair understanding of what is going on in the minds on either side of the fence.

I think the worst agony is somebody being denied the bliss and comforts of family life. The soldiers do get occasional peace postings, but most of the time they live a separated life and their tenuous link with the normal life is the generous leave allowed to them. Free rations and special pay and allowances that they get, do compensate them to a degree for having to maintain two establishments, but not the emotional stress and the occupational hazards. For this, they need a special consideration from the nation in some visible form. Such an elating upsurge comes their way briefly from the common man during the war periods.

Otherwise, my civilian friends carry the impression that they are in the military profession because they, in any case, were unfit to come good in civil careers. So, they perforce had to choose the next best option i.e. the army life. Sadly, it is hardly ever appreciated that some sons of this nation have to come forward to defend our soil, unless we are prepared to be driven to the position of some sort of a 'White Man`s Burden' again. Soldiers produce the precious wealth of peace without which all our dreams of development and material prosperity can simply end up in smoke.

Once I tried to bring home to a young police officer what it meant to lead one thousand men in battle by a colonel. He told me rather innocently that he had often handled four thousand men placed at his disposal in his police lines to deal with the law and order situations in his district. I had to tell him plainly that handling was a bit different from commanding. An army major, with twice his service, just commanded a company of hundred men. But, if an occasion so demanded, he could move his men over a minefield, covered by the enemy machineguns spitting fire.

Again, in a social gathering, a senior army major tried to speak to the local deputy commissioner on equal terms. The D.C. who did not take very kindly to it tersely reminded the major that he was somewhere in between his brigadier and major general and he should be spoken to accordingly. It is really here that the shoe pinches. Why should a civil officer, with just about six years of service, take precedence over an army brigadier, with well over twenty years of standing, especially when he has reached the position after undergoing two selections? Does it not convey an impression that military is meant to be a subordinate service? Even the British who ruled us though their D.C.' s had assigned precedence to these officials outside their districts below the lieutenant colonels.

All this leaves me wondering, if this is what goes by the name of civil superiority in our democratic system! If it is really so, the idea is deeply flawed and it needs to be urgently revisited.

(A reproduction from the writer's article in 'The Tribune' of 16.7.2009.)

20. THAT EID OF 1857

It was the destined day of 1st August, 1857—the holy day of Bakr Eid. Frederic Cooper, the then Deputy Commissioner of Amritsar celebrated it in style at Ajnala by slaughtering 282 disarmed men of the 26th Native Infantry Regiment. Pandeys, Tiwaris and Mishras were shot through their hearts at point blank range and thus, as he says, were 'launched into eternity'. The dead and dying were then dumped by the village sweepers into a dry well close to the Ajnala police station.

After the ghastly exploit, Cooper felt that he had truly written himself in to the colonial history and deserved a pedestal in the Trafalgar Square by the side of Admiral Nelson. After all, 'England expected every Englishman to do his duty' and he, 'a single Anglo-Saxon' on the spot had done his admirably by coldly presiding over so memorable an execution. His claim to fame deserves to be studied in the perspective of the times. The incident also brings in to correct focus, the value that the British colonialists then attached to human rights when their own interests were threatened.

As the times tick, the fortunes fluctuate. The eighteenth & nineteenth centuries belonged to the British. Having truly emerged as the 'super people' in the world then, they had begun to entertain, rather imprudently, the illusions of permanence about this transitory phenomenon. Convinced that they were born to be the masters, the British thought that the 'natives' everywhere should be grateful to the 'Whiteman' for bringing to them the light of civilization. Lord Macaulay, the erudite law member of the Governor `s General Council, boasted that 'a single shelf of a good European library was worth the whole literature of India and Arabia', in total regard of the facts that India had given the world its first book, the 'Rig Veda' and Arabia had triggered the first wave of Renaissance in Europe.

Their insatiable lust to own the world, ruthless exploitation of the colonies, interference in the way of life of the subjugated people and the humiliation inflicted on the locally recruited army men ultimately exploded in India in the form of a great revolt, spearheaded by the native soldiery in 1857. Strangely enough, Punjab has been projected in a rather poor light in relation to the 1857 Revolt, though all parts of the province from Peshawar, Kohat and Dera Ghazi

Khan in the west and Ambala, Gurgaon and Rewari to the east gave full vent to their anger against the alien. The only exception to this were the the Phulkian states who, for reason of their history, half-heartedly collaborated with the British regime. In the recent past, they had just escaped being annexed by Maharaja Ranjit Singh because of the active British help and thus felt beholden to them. The rest of Punjab, including the Sikh contingents at Benaras, Mhow and Jhansi enthusiastically participated in the great patriotic upsurge and later paid a heavy price for it. It is a fact of history (though not a very prominent one) that two native regiments at Ambala had rebelled almost simultaneously when the first spark of the Revolt got ignited at Meerut on the 10th of May, 1857.

Now reverting to the grand ceremonial sacrifice at Ajnala, the events run like this. At the first signs of trouble in the province, the Chief Commissioner of Punjab wrote to the local authorities the "tone and temper of the native soldiery in general and of the 'Purbea' elements in particular, should be closely watched and prompt action should be taken at the first symptoms of violent spirit. The 'hindustanies' should not be trusted to the posts of respect and responsibility.

In compliance with this directive, the 26th Native Infantry Regiment located at Mian Mir was disarmed on 13th May and confined to the barracks. This open display of distrust sent a clear message to the sepoys that no loyalty was expected of them. Frustrated by their prolonged idleness and enraged over their humiliation at the hands of the overbearing 'firinghee' officers, they ultimately burst forth from their barracks on 30th July. Prakash Pandey, one of the mutineers, rushed menacingly towards Major Spencer. Upon this, a contingent of confused Sikh irregulars opened indiscriminate fire which scattered the unarmed sepoys. Major Spencer and the sergeant major who had rushed to his help were killed.

The general direction of escape of the sepoys could not be immediately ascertained as a sudden dust storm had greatly reduced the visibility in the area. However, the next day by noon, the tehsildar of Ajnala conveyed to Fredric Cooper that a large body of 'purbeas' was sighted near Doodean on the bank of river Ravi and he was rushing to the place with the available police force. The police personnel with the tehsildar immediately opened fire as soon as the fugitives were sighted. The fatigued sepoys were in no position to fight back with their bare hands. The flooded river behind them further worked to their disadvantage. In desperation, they plunged themselves into the river and some of them got washed away, but many of them made to an island in the river which was rapidly shrinking and submerging under the rising level of the river.

By about 5 P.M., Cooper arrived on the scene, accompanied by his aide and an assortment of irregular troops, mostly from Tiwana and Sandawala families. Only two boats were available to capture the escapees and bring them ashore. The famished and fatigued sepoys did not put up any resistance, though quite a few of them jumped into the flooded river and got drowned to the great relief of Cooper. The others surrendered in the hope of a fair trial through court martial. After all, a large bulk of them was innocent and they had fled in face of indiscriminate firing on them. Myriad patterns of the kind formed by the moonlight in the puddles of water, were assuming shape in Cooper's mind also, unknown to the captives. He had, in fact, already sent orders for a firing squad of fifty to be sent to Ajnala before leaving Amritsar.

In all 214 were taken prisoners by Cooper and brought to Ajnala police station around midnight. Another batch of 66 was brought before day break. They had to be confined in the bastion of the tehsil building as no more space was available at the police station. Preparations for their execution got under way immediately. A deep dry well close to the police station was earmarked to dump the corpses. Village sweepers were summoned to drag the bodies of the 'dishonoured and crime-stained soldiery' to their mass grave.

When August 1, 1857, the holy day of Bakr Eid, dawned the unfortunate humans were brought before the firing squads in batches of ten for being shot through their hearts. The cool and collected Cooper could note with great interest the stoic calmness on their faces. A few who refused to walk before the firing squads were dragged to the place in the manner of sacrificial goats for being shot on the ground. By 10 A.M. 237 of them 'had met their doom'. Then came the news that the 45 still left were refusing to come out of the tehsil bastion. The soldiers at Cooper`s disposal rushed to drag the defiant men to his musketeers only to find them suffocated to death or lying unconscious. Overcrowding, the summer heat and paucity of air in the securely locked dingy room had taken their toll.

Nonetheless, Cooper did not have to bother for all this. Rather this had simplified the things for him. The sweepers were ordered to dump the dead and the unconscious in the well. It was then filled with lime and charcoal to ensure quick melting of their flesh. A mound of earth was raised over the well. Cooper felt very gratified that the villagers named the spot by an urdu word, 'moofsidar', which translated in to English as the 'rebels` hole'.

The ghost of Cooper is perhaps still hovering around at the sacrificial spot, craving for immortality for his gory enactment there even after over one and a half centuries. History may one day like to grant his wish, but not as a hero of the British Empire, but as the 'Butcher of Ajnala'.

(A reproduction from the writer's article in 'The Statesman' on 9.9.1995.)

(B) NAVY

The Protectors of the Seas Surrounding Us

21. INDIA'S RIGHTS IN THE SURROUNDING SEAS

On 11th February, 1998, a contingent of troops from our army, navy, air force and coast guard carried out a swift operation, code-named 'Ops Leech', close to the coast of one of our islands in the Andaman and Nicobar cluster. This resulted in the capture of a small flotilla of four trawlers and boats carrying a sizeable cache of arms and ammunition. The haul included some highly sophisticated military grade weapons like rocket launchers, heavy machine guns (possibly for use in anti-aircraft role) and an assortment of rifles and pistols. The seventy four gun-runners who were captured could not be immediately identified and what they were up to also remained to be ascertained. However, it could be surmised that the fleet came somewhere from the south-east Asia and its cargo was meant for the insurgents active in the north-east of our country.

The defence forces involved in the operation, especially the military intelligence, certainly deserved to be complimented for this success. However, in some quarters, the operation raised the visions of India discharging a regional responsibility as a sub-continental power. To some, the incident brought to mind what we had done a few years back in Sri Lanka and Maldives. In fact, nothing in the nature of any extra-territorial exercise of authority had taken place here. The event should have more appropriately drawn a parallel with the Purulia arms drop mystery.

We do not have any illusions of being the international policemen. In fact, no nation should entertain such pretentions. Any such authority can only rise out of international agreements or the directions from the U.N. Security Council.

However, we do have some territorial rights that run deep in the Bay of Bengal and the Arabian Sea. Some discussion on the law of seas seems necessary at this stage so that the Andaman incident is seen in the correct perspective. In the sixteenth century, the Portuguese enjoyed considerable maritime supremacy. To checkmate them, a Dutchman, Hugo Grotius, propounded the theory of 'Mare Librum' i.e. the open seas. He argued that movable property was capable of being seized and an immovable one was at least capable of being enclosed. In any case, all property was in the nature of an exhaustible asset. Thus, the seas not having any of the attributes of 'property' could not be 'owned'. Consequently, seas should remain open to all as the international watery highways.

The mastery over the seas having passed on to the Britain in the eighteenth century, Seldon, a British, felt emboldened to come up with the alternate doctrine of 'Mare Clausum', according to which the adjacent seas could be appropriated, subject to the others being allowed a peaceful passage through them.

Our concepts about the seas have undergone a change since the days of Grotius. The oceans are not only the conduits of wealth, but also the repositories of boundless wealth themselves, in the form of fish, salt, petroleum and a variety of minerals. These are certainly worth appropriating, if one can. To begin with, a belt of three nautical miles along the coast, based on the range of cannon shots of the time, came to be considered as a natural prolongation of a country's sovereignty into the neighbouring seas. Some nations, however, went absolutely wild over the width of this territorial belt and declared as much as two hundred miles of the adjacent oceans as their exclusive property.

There was, thus, a clear need for coming to some international understanding to minimize the potential conflicts on this count. A number of conferences were held under the aegis of the United Nations to thrash out some solution to the global problem. Finally, the Third U.N. Convention on the Law of Sea appointed a seabed committee which produced a monumental document, The U.N. Convention on the Law of Sea, in 1982. As per the U.N. Convention, countries can extend their sovereignty to the adjacent seas to the extent of twelve nautical miles measured from the low tide baseline. This zone is called 'territorial waters'. The country concerned can exercise sovereign jurisdiction in this zone, subject to the right of others to a peaceful passage. Such passage means that there should be no suspicious halts, submarines stand bound to appear on the surface and fly appropriate flag and the ships have to pre-notify their arrival (some countries, however, insist on prior approval for their entry).

Next to the territorial waters, the Convention provides for another twelve nautical miles to be called a 'contiguous zone'. The jurisdiction of a country in this belt is restricted to the fiscal, customs and sanitation related matters. Our country has, however, notified its right to intervene in this area on count of the security concerns also. Besides, the countries have also been permitted to have a two hundred nautical miles wide economic zone exclusive to them. The littoral states have yet another entitlement in the neighbouring seas—their continental shelf i.e. the natural prolongation of their territory up to a certain depth. However, under the Convention, a country cannot claim shelf wider than 350 miles from its baseline or 100 hundred miles from the 2500 metres isobaths (a line connecting points 2500 metres deep), though it can always claim a shelf 200 hundred miles wide.

We are lucky in matters maritime. Besides commanding sea routes in all directions, our continental shelf extends as far as five hundred miles in some areas. As against ours, the U.S. shelf is just 20 to 254 miles in the east and mere 1 to 50 miles on its west coast. We are thus a geographically advantaged country. Beyond the permitted continental shelf, lie the high seas that are the common heritage of the mankind and can be freely exploited by everybody on benefit sharing basis under proper licence from the world body.

Article 297 of our Constitution places all lands, minerals and other things of value under our territorial waters and continental shelf in the ownership of the Union. The Maritime Zones Act, 1976, declares our position with regard to our territorial waters, contiguous zones, exclusive economic zones and the continental shelf. The act also lays down the extent of our authority and rights in these maritime belts. Thus, what our troops did near Andaman on 11th February, 1998 was just a routine and rightful exercise of our sovereign authority.

(A reproduction from the writer' s article in 'The Hindustan Times' of 3.3.1998.)

22. LIVING HISTORY

Commodore Babru Bahan Yadav, Mahavir Chakra, "the man who led the charge on Karachi in our war with Pakistan in 1971"—this is how our then Naval Chief, Admiral S.M. Nanda, has referred to him, though the Commodore, on his part, would like to give lion's share of credit for this first offensive operation of the Indian Navy to the Admiral himself.

A city within a city is fast coming up to the south-west of our national capital by the name of Dwarka. Sector 2 of this sub-city has an old-age home suggestively named "Godhuli" that alludes to the dusty setting when cows return home raising dust. The place is meant to provide comfort to the people in the evening of their life. Commodore Yadav is one of the occupants of this senior citizens' home.

Our shipping, no doubt, once ruled the waves both to our West and East. Tragically, however, seas were to be our weakness for many centuries thereafter. In fact, a perception prevailed in our minds for a long while that crossing seas was a sin. When Akbar the Great was face to face with the majesty of the sea for the first time on his conquest of Gujarat, he reacted like a child taken to Disneyland. The mighty Aurangzeb paid protection money to the Portuguese for safety of the royal ladies sailing for Hajj. In line with this ethos, our Navy was not assigned any operational task during our wars in 1962 and 1965. Our brave sailors carried a sore inside on this count.

Thus, when another war broke out with Pakistan in 1971, our Naval chief had a point to prove. It was decided to go straight at the jugular vein of the Pakistan Navy i.e. their assets at Karachi. Three missile boats — Nipat, Nirghat and Veer — were deputed to mount the attack. Two Petya class ships were earmarked to accompany them mainly for air cover. This was no Armada of any sort, but a lean and mean sneak force, highly vulnerable to air attack and the coastal batteries of Karachi equipped with 16 inch calibre guns.

Against all odds, the task force managed to slip within the striking distance of Karachi. Its missiles then let loose a hell on the harbour, setting its oil storage tanks ablaze, besides sinking or crippling around half a dozen war ships, including the two Pakistan Navy destroyers— Haider and Shahjehan. All this forced the Pakistan Navy to forget about any offensive designs on our shores. They instead decided to sit in the safety of their harbour.

The brave Commodore (then a commander) who, thus, wrote himself in our naval history in this operation has finally dropped anchor in "Godhuli" to enjoy the twilight years of his life.

After all, every life has an evening to it, unless some unnatural causes deprive it of this delight.

(A reproduction from the writer's article in 'The Tribune' of 25.2.2005.)

23. A LIFE CHECK-MATED

Captain V.P. Laroia , a retired officer from the Indian Navy, was in his mid-eighties when I told him a joke about one nonagenarian John. The old man was floating around in a party animatedly when the host introduced him to the gathering, "Mr. John. Though in his nineties, he is still full of life". The jovial John clarified, as if in protest, "In early nineties, you see". This left the guests peeling with laughter, but nobody missed the throb of life in his words. Not to be outdone by John and taking the joke a step forward, the Captain added that, in his case, he was not ninety even. Sadly, he was never to be. He died recently when he was around 85.

Captain Laroia was the first among us to make grade for commission in the Indian armed forces. What an occasion it was when he left for his pre-commission training in New Castle in England! As the Muslim devotees returning from Hajj are called 'Haji`s', the people coming back after a trip to England were then given the appellation of 'England-Returned'. After he had broken the glass ceiling, many of us, including me, made our way through it to get to the commissioned ranks in the three services. One of us, Air Chief Marshall Satish Sareen went on to rise to the high position of the Air Chief of the country. Captain Laroia was selected by the late Federal Service Commission and was Admiral Tahliani`s batch-mate. He stood every chance of moving higher in the naval hierarchy, but decided instead to retire early in the interest of his family.

He had lost his father, a doctor, quite early in his life. Untimely demise of father left him saddled with the huge responsibility of four unmarried sisters and two brothers. The brave sailor settled all his siblings with loving care one by one, in the best traditions of a dutiful son.

After all this was over, he was still left with the task of taking care of his three daughters. All of them came up as highly accomplished girls. But, they were daughters nevertheless. Nobody understood it better than he what it took to settle daughters in our society. So, he left his job and joined a German shipping concern to accumulate some money for ensuring a decent married life for his daughters.

It was only after all the three girls were also nicely settled that he started thinking for himself and his loving wife who had stood by him in all his struggles. He now ensconced himself in his single-storey bungalow at Chandigarh, sprawling over two kanals. It had a very moderate plinth area. The rest of the plot was covered with fruit-bearing trees, grassy lawns, laced with flowery plants and a big kitchen garden. The couple now spent their time in solace tending the trees and plants with delicate care.

Besides, the Captain took to the game of chess. He would put an advertisement in the local papers inviting people to play with him. After a while, he was able to locate a keen and likable partner to play with right till the end of his life. The two were often seen playing the game with great gusto and occasionally, quarreling noisily over the moves. In the end, death check-mated him while he was playing the final game of chess on his lap-top. He died sweetly in the manner of a person going to sleep. His face reflected serenity and satisfaction of a life lived well and meaningfully.

(A reproduction from the writer's article in 'The Tribune' of 19.4.2013.)

(C) CENTRAL RESERVE POLICE FORCE

The peace-keepers to the nation

24. THE HIGH TASK OF KEEPING THE COUNTRY TOGETHER

It is the year 1988 and the venue is Brahmbuta Akhara in Amritsar overlooking the Golden Temple complex. The temperature is touching 47 degree Celsius. Two C.R.P. Force jawans with big patches of perspiration on their uniform are manning a Light Machine Gun post atop the building. The post has a few C.G.I. sheets as overhead cover. There is an announcement on the public address system exhorting the militants holed inside to surrender. The C.R.P.F. men instinctively take cover. There is a spontaneous burst of AK 47 fire on the post. This is the militant's reply to the suggestion of surrender. The Jawans are apparently unmindful of the firing on them. Having lived with the hissing bullets for years on end, they now know that the bullets hurt only when these hit.

Winning appreciation and applause here, suffering criticism and casualties there, the C.R.P.F. men seem to go on and on. Their staying power is simply amazing. Wherever there is trouble C.R.P.F. is always around. Freedom and democracy have brought our people the right to dissent after the slavery of centuries. There is an unmistakable and overpowering urge in the country to come good in the new situation. However, our general approach has been too excessively agitative for comfort. It seems that we have awakened to our rights but not to our duties. The fear of the law is largely gone, but respect for the law is yet to take roots in our psyche.

For the police in general and the C.R.P. Force in particular, all this has meant an intense strain on nerves and resources. Since the epicenter of trouble keeps shifting in the country, the state police forces get a periodic opportunity to return to their barracks. However, as peace returns to a place, the C.R.P.F. shifts to the new front to fight its next battle against lawlessness. The Force thus remains perpetually locked in operations. It has now known no rest for ages.

The vice-regal outfit of yesteryears has already expanded from just one battalion of the Crown Representative's Police to around two hundred and thirty battalions of the Central Reserve Police Force. Still, however, a little reserve that is temporarily created on every expansion to give some respite to the Force gets sucked into operations in no time.

Over the years the Force has dealt with the dacoit gangs, underground insurgents, Naxalite extremists, agitators, anti-social elements, terrorists and in fact, trouble makers of all hues. In addition, it has given and drawn first blood in most of our post-Independence wars and border skirmishes.

Describing the C.R.P. Force as the unsung hero of the 1971 war, the war correspondent of 'The Indian Express' reported that the Force did not yield even a single square inch of the Pakistan territory entrusted to it by the Army.

In 1958, a patrol from the Force led by Karam Singh, the legendary D.C.I.O. of the Intelligence Bureau (Incidentally, later his three sons were also to serve in the Force), tore through the snows along an uncharted route to the Aksai Chin road. This death defying band was the first and the only one to have a ground level look at the road and to bring along invaluable evidence about the surreptitiously built road.

Later, on 21st October, 1959, the opening shots of the Indo-Chinese war were exchanged between a platoon of the C.R.P.F. and a much bigger contingent of the Chinese army on the banks of the river Chang Chenmo, two miles to the west of Kongka La in Ladakh. Despite being hopelessly outnumbered by three companies of the Chinese army who took them by surprise, the C.R.P.F. sub-unit fought manfully, killing an officer and injuring some other ranks of the enemy. Ten C.R.P.F. men also fell martyrs in the action and the survivors could be captured only when they had fired their last bullet. 21st October has since become a day of homage to the police martyrs all over the country.

Similarly, in 1965, a detachment from the 2nd Battalion of the Force valiantly fought back the onslaught of a regular Pakistan army brigade in the Rann of Kutchch. The Pakistan brigade commander suffered a sack for having failed to dislodge the C.R.P.F. detachment from the defensive position, despite having an armoured column in support of his attack. In 1971 war with Pakistan, the Force again cornered considerable glory in the 'Chicken Neck' area. A war correspondent of 'The Indian Express' while referring to the Force as an 'unsung hero of the war', reported that the Force did not yield even a single inch of the Pakistan territory left to its care by our Army.

In fact, the C.R.P.F. history is brimming with the events and exploits of this genre. Its 88th Mahila Battalion, the first female combat unit of the country, opened its account of battle honours with a 'Sena Medal' in Sri Lanka (Now it has since been able to add many more laurels to its illustrious history, including the most coveted 'Ashok Chakra').

The Border Security Force and the Indo-Tibetan Border Police are now the worthy heirs to the glorious legacy of the C.R.P.F. on the Indo-Pakistan and the Indo-Chinese borders of the country. Nonetheless, there is hardly any doubt that the Force would again be summoned to fight side by side with our Army in the next 'nation-at-war' situation and it would never be found wanting in any of the multi-dimensional roles entrusted to it.

In the area of internal security, the C.R.P.F.'s role has been equally laudable. The Force has made a very considerable contribution in keeping the country together. The C.R.P.F. Act of 1949 defines the general duties of a member of the Force to be "to obey and execute all orders and warrants lawfully issued to him by any competent authority, to detect and bring offenders to justice and to apprehend all persons whom he is legally authorized to apprehend and for whose apprehension sufficient grounds exist". The Force has, however, been performing much beyond the call of its normal duties right from the day of its raising.

The C.R.P.F. men can wield lathis, handle tear smoke and fire machine guns and mortars with equal ease. They pose minimum problems to the borrowing authorities and are serviceable to the maximum. The Force is, in every way, a S.P.'s delight. To borrow Brig. Dalvi's words, 'they are tigers in action and dogs in obedience'.

Since the last Fifties, the Force always had its hands full. The Intelligence Bureau was able to milk out a company strength of the Force to show flag at the new forward locations in Ladakh in 1959 with great difficulty. In the Sixties and Seventies the Force was involved neck deep in operations against the underground insurgents in the North-eastern states and the Naxalites in West Bengal, Andhra Pradesh and Kerala etc. In mid-Eighties terrorism raised its ugly head in Punjab. Here it was not merely a situation of law and order, but that of a covert war. The hostile neighbour to our west had not only succeeded in putting militancy in the heads of our misguided youth, but also AK 47's in their hands to kill their compatriots. The Punjab police for a while was unprepared to deal with this explosive situation adequately. The formidable staying power of the C.R.P.F. provided the much-needed breathing time to the state police to come in to its own.

Vigil from a bivouac

The temporarily sick state of Punjab soon returned to its radiant health. Its police force could now hope to have some much needed and well-deserved respite in barracks. As regards the C.R.P.F. questions soon came to be asked as to what the Force was doing in peaceful Punjab. Similarly, when peace returns to Kashmir and the bleeding valley starts breathing normally and regains its lost paradise, the C.R.P.F. would be packing its bags to move to the next trouble spot to fight its next battle. (Presently, it is locked in a mortal combat with the Naxalites in Chhatisgarh, Jharkhand, Odisha, Bihar, Maharashtra and elsewhere.)

(A reproduction from the writer's article in 'The Times of India' on 28.12.1993.)

25. THE ROAD THROUGH AKSAI CHIN

On 21st October every year, policemen all over the country stand in solemn silence to pay homage to the police martyrs in front of their memorials. This was the day when a C.R.P. Force platoon valiantly fought an unequal battle with a three company strong Chinese army contingent at Hot Springs in Ladakh in 1959. After the battle of Haldi Ghati in 1576 AD between the vastly superior forces of the Emperor Akbar and the rag tag army of Maharana Pratap Singh, this is the second occasion where the glory goes to the vanquished rather than the winner. Ten of our jawans fell martyrs on the spot and many others sustained serious bullet injuries. With that exploded the myth of the 'Hindi-Chini, Bhai Bhai'

Just a year earlier, the C.R.P.F. men deployed at Leh were involved in an exploit that many would envy, but few dare. By this time the Tibet-Sinkiang road surreptitiously built by the Chinese through our Aksai Chin region, roughly along the 'Silk Route' of the olden days, had become operational. It left Tibet near Lanak La and entered Sinkiang at Haji Langar. The Government of India wanted to send a suitable protest note to China over this issue. But before that it was necessary to be sure about the fact that the road violated our territory.

It was thus decided to send two patrols to verify the ground realities about the road. The Chinese convoys were then reported to be plying regularly on the highway. The area astride the road was also simmering with the Chinese soldiers. So, it meant penetrating behind the enemy lines. Still bigger peril lay in getting lost in the vast solitude of the snows,

All this notwithstanding, the two patrols left their bases, defying death and dangers, sometimes in the middle of 1958. One patrol party consisted exclusively of our army personnel under Lt. Iyengar. This patrol was to get to Haji Langar in north Aksai Chin where the road cuts in to the Indian territory. They were to then move towards south on or astride the road for some distance and then return by the same route. Overcoming a multitude of difficulties the intrepid patrol did reach Haji Langar, but was unfortunately captured by the Chinese as soon as it moved southwards. The party was released at Karakoram pass when the Indian government protested.

The other patrol was drawn from the C.R.P.F. sub-unit deployed at Leh to police the Indo-Tibetan border. The mission was led by Karam Singh, the legendary D.C.I.O. from the Intelligence Bureau. The patrol had two options with regard to the route. It could penetrate to Lanak La in Tibet and then proceed north to explore the road. This idea had to be abandoned as it involved intruding into the Chinese territory and the chances of the patrol getting captured also ran high. The second option was to proceed east from Shamul Lungpa and to hit the road somewhere near Sarigh Jilganang Kol. This meant crossing two mountain ranges 18000 to 20000 feet high, but the route lay entirely in our claimed territory.

Some preparatory action had already been taken to support the move of this party, in that secret supply dumps had already been created at Hot Springs and Shamul Lungpa on the way. Reaching Shamul Lungpa in itself was not an easy task but from there onwards it was a real unearthly endeavour. Struggling against the elements that threatened life at every step, the patrol pushed on with a crusader's zeal. After crossing the first mountain range the party got on to the second. They now had the view of the Sarigh Jilganang lake. Coming down they saw the signs of the Chinese movement in the area. There were heavy track marks on one side of the lake. Obviously the Chinese vehicles had been driven to the lake to collect water.

Karam Singh and his gallant men then traversed the road. They moved some distance to the north and south astride it and collected conclusive evidence that it passed through our territory. A Chinese convoy was seen moving on the road. It was secretly photographed from the hideout of the patrol. On their way back, the patrol also uprooted a wooden milestone from the road and brought it as a souvenir. An amazing exploit thus came to an end. The dare devils were back to the base after writing a saga on the snows of Aksai Chin.

Next year it was decided to establish some new forward posts in Ladakh to checkmate the any further onslaught of the Chinese on our territories. The C.R.P.F. company at Leh was placed at the disposal of Karam Singh to execute this plan which later came to known as the 'Forward Policy'. The sub-unit thus moved from Leh and established a platoon post at Tsogatsalu on 17 October, 1959. On October 19, it established a firm base at Hot Springs. Next day a small reconnaissance party, having one constable and a local civilian, was sent to Kongka La where the next post was to be located. When this party did not return, Karam Singh left Hot Springs on 21st October with a platoon of twenty personnel to search out the missing patrol. This platoon fell into an elaborately laid Chinese ambush on the bank of river Chang Chenmo about two miles west of Kongka La. Eight men of the patrol were killed in the first flush, but the rest returned the fire which accounted for a Chinese commander and injured a few others.

The surviving C.R.P.F. men could be captured only when they had fired their last bullet. One badly injured constable who could not be easily carried was cruelly bayoneted to death by the Chinese. The final toll was the ten precious lives. This incident marks a watershed in the Indo-Chinese relations. The Chinese finally released Karam Singh and the captured C.R.P.F. personnel on 30th November, along with the bodies of the dead. The Chinese Prime Minister , Chu Enlai, then on an official visit to India, even met Karam Singh in the hospital to enquire about his wellbeing. However, after this, the fond slogan of 'Hindi Chini, Bhai Bhai' acquired a rather sinister ring about it. It was decided to stop forward patrolling and stick to somewhat better defensible positions in depth.

(A reproduction from the writer's article in the 'Hindustan Times' on 20. 10.1991.)

26. THE MARTYERS WHO GOT SHORT-CHANGED

Our Bodo tribesmen have their settlements sparsely dotting the Himalayan foothills in Assam. They have been agitating for quite a while to have a separate state of Bodoland. Their biggest concentration is in Kokrajhar. Their struggle till the early part of 1974 had been peaceful. Somehow, they felt that they had not been making much headway through peaceful means. So they suddenly decided on a violent course to achieve their aim.

I was then the second-in-command of the 21st Battalion, CRPF, located in the area and my commandant, A.K. Bandopadhyay, was away on some assignment. I received a wireless message from the town of Sidli that our men had suffered a surprise attack by the Bodos and two of them had fallen martyrs. Many others had been injured and one of the injured was in a critical state. I rushed to the place to be among them in the hour of their grief.

I learnt on the spot that the Bodo agitators had gathered in the area in quite some number with a violent intent about which nobody had any clue. In fact, the local S.H.O., a well-intentioned old man, got into their midst to argue with them about their dispersal. He did not realise that this time, they had not gathered to disperse peacefully. When he persisted, they fell upon him. Finding him in grave danger of being cruelly lynched, three C.R.P. F. men waded through the violent mob to rescue him.

Finding no other way to save the man, constables Purnima Munda and Hridaya Narain provided him body cover and another constable Kesho Rao Pattar also made a desperate dash to reach him. Munda and Narain had their helmets removed and given mortal blows on their head with *'daos'*. Pattar also had his skull badly fractured, but he survived to our pleasant surprise. However, my other boys, though also under assault, recovered quickly and fired a few rounds to make the blood-thirsty mob to disperse.

While camping at the site, my Commandant and the D.I.G. also joined me. We were of the view that it was not merely a case of gallantry but of martyrdom on the part of Munda and Narain. We made out a case for the award of Ashoka Chakra to them posthumously, while Pattar was proposed for the President's Police Medal for Gallantry. The Assam government put its entire weight behind our citations.

Sadly, however, a discriminatory rule happened to be in place at the time that said that those authorised Police Medals (that have woefully low precedence) could not get higher awards like the Ashoka, Kirti and Shaurya Chakras. This deprived the two C.R.P.F. martyrs of their due and highly deserved recognition and they finally ended up with the President's Police Medals for Gallantry, along with Pattar. Our Force was thus left poorer by two highly cherished Ashoka Chakras, merely because of an irrational stipulation that had somehow escaped the government attention.

(A reproduction from the writer's article in 'The Tribune' of 29.7.2011.)

27. THEIR HOUR OF AGONY

A C.R.P.F. patrol in its area of operations

I have served with three of the elite armed forces of the country — the Army, the National Security Guard and Central Reserve Police Force. Each one of them is peerless in its field. Though I parted company with them many decades ago, I still follow them in their triumphs and travails. I often feel that I have left something of me behind with them. The highly surgical operation by the N.S.G. in Mumbai in 2008 fills me with pride. When I read about the Army casualties in Kashmir, I anxiously look for the cost they inflicted on the terrorist in turn.

I had the longest tenure in the CRPF, which today is in the throes of agony, having lost 76 of its jawans in Dantewada. Sadly, this district in Chhattisgarh is again in the news owing to the massacre of 36 persons, including 12 Special Police Officers, by Maoists. It is not the loss of the gallant men that rankles with the CRPF personnel — the lives of all the three hundred thousand of them are on pledge to the nation. The sad part of it is that this time they could not make their martyrdom count. Their sacrifice seems to have gone largely in vain, and has rather attracted adverse comment from certain quarters that are hardly in the know of things.

I have commanded half a dozen battalions of this force one after the other. I never had to look back while leading operations. I always knew that my men would be following right behind me, for they are not the ones who would flee in the face of danger. They have after all fought the Pakistan and the Chinese armies in highly adverse situations, giving and drawing the first blood.

In Dantewada, however, they got little opportunity to show their mettle. Explosives laid on the road and the sudden hail of bullets from the surrounding high ground sealed their fate. This reminds me of the plight of Brigadier Dalvi's 7th Infantry Brigade in the Thagla Ridge area of NEFA in 1962 and that of the French Army trapped at Dien Bien Phu in Vietnam in 1954. I can assure you that in their situation nobody, not even the American, Israeli and our own army would have done any better. The only question that remains to be answered is: how so many heavily armed insurgents could collect in the area without getting noticed.

Anyway, nothing much is lost so long as the will to fight is intact. Our jawans understand it well that those who live by the sword, some of them have to die by the sword. Their difficulty is that the Maoists who they face are our own people. There is, therefore, no question of carrying revenge on mind while dealing with them. They have, thus, a difficult fight on their hands indeed, but they would get even with the believers in violence soon.

The old hands like me would like to tell them that it is not possible to tear an inconvenient page from out of history. However, a few glorious ones can always be added to make it fade.

(A reproduction from the writer's article in 'The Tribune' of 20.5.2010)

28. A GREAT DOER

In my view, post Independence India has produced only six real 'Bharat Ratna`s'. They are M.S. Swaminathan, Sam Pitroda, Dr. Kurien Verghese, M.M.Suri, Dr. E. Shreedharan and, of course, Dr.Manmohan Singh. Maankombu Sambasivan Swaminathan ushered the 'Green Revolution' in the country. Earlier, we used be standing permanently with a begging bowl before the Americans to feed our hungry through the PL 48 arrangement. Satyanarayan Gangaram Petroda revolutionised the tele-communication networks of the nation. But for the timely 'White Revolution' of Dr.Verghese Kurien, we would have been drinking milk made out of urea and detergents. Diesel engines manufactured all over the world, including our own locomotives at Chitranjan, have the transmission system invented by Er. M.M.Suri. Dr. Elattuvalapil Shreedharan has brought us the Konkan Railway and the Metro networks that are the pride of the nation. By Dr. Manmohan Singh as the 'Bharat Ratna', of course, I mean the vintage Finance Minister who salvaged our nearly sunk economy in the closing years of the last century.

Most of our bureaucrats, undoubtedly, pass their time holding conferences over coffee and cashew nuts and doing hardly anything of substance. There is, indeed, a sprinkling of some brilliant bureaucrats here and there who are somehow keeping the wheels of the government moving, while being often hidden from view themselves.

One among such 'Mini-ratna`s was late R.N. Sheopory, the former Director General of the Central Reserve Police Force who sorted out many festering problems of the Force during his tenure at the helm. A large bulk of our senior scale officers was then holding their ranks in ad hoc capacity because of the seniority disputes between the ex-Army and the directly appointed officers. Nobody wished to hold this hot potato in hand. I, during my short tenure as the establishment officer, had left a note in the relevant file which was a key to the solution of this problem. Mr. Sheopory took pains to read this note and made up his mind instantly. No time was lost in obtaining government approval and orders were flashed overnight regularising all the ad hoc promotions to the great relief of the officer cadre.

Similarly, the issue of giving combatant ranks to our ministerial staff had been hanging fire for years. Whenever, the options were invited from the staff, the opinions were understandably divided. Securing unanimity on the point was impracticable. Mr. Sheopory instructed his staff officers to prepare a log of all the 38 conferences held over the matter. This log clearly showed that the things were coming to Square One after every five to six meetings.

After maneuvering clearance from the Law Ministry that this could be done, he gate-crashed into the Ministry of Home Affairs leaving no room for them to defer the decision by holding yet another conference.

Another gift that he gave to the Force was the Risk Premia Scheme, an internal insurance arrangement for all ranks. Next in line with him was the formation of a proper cadre for the Force officers on lines of the other central services. Sadly, he did not live long enough to see this goal achieved. Nonetheless, the great doer died the death of a soldier with his boots on.

(A reproduction from the writer's article in the 'The Tribune' of 11.10.2012.)

29. A BRUSH WITH HISTORY AT CHIKMAGLUR

The C.R.P.F. advance party arriving at Chikmaglur

Chikmaglur is a small sleepy town of Karnataka, nestling in the scenic splendour of the Western Ghats. Its sprawling coffee and cardamom plantations and its petite girls smiling and talking their way through the town give it a touch of serenity and wellbeing. Centuries had been tiptoeing past this sleeping beauty, taking care not to wake it up. Then, the town suddenly 'woke one morning and found itself famous'. That was the day Indira Gandhi announced her candidature for a seat in our Lok Sabha through Chikmaglur constituency.

The Janata Party government at the Centre was keen to induct the C.R.P. Force at the place to ensure orderly election, while the Congress government in the state was against this deployment. The irony behind the whole thing was that a Constitutional amendment, made a little while back by the Congress government itself then in power at New Delhi, provided for induction of the central armed forces in the states and for these forces to work under the directions of the central government.

Nonetheless, a weird accident at the town of Ujire in which an innocent school girl, Gayathri, lost her life, after having been hit by a tear-smoke shell fired during a local police action, built enough public pressure on the state government to requisition the C.R.P.

Force. Moreover, one legal view floating around then was that the Force, if requisitioned by the state, would have to work under its directions. Besides, the Election Commission was also of the opinion that the induction of the C.R.P. Force was necessary in the interest of the smooth and fair conduct of the election. It was under these circumstances that the 51st and 5th Battalions of the C.R.P. Force were rushed to the constituency at the very last moment.

My unit, the 51st Battalion received orders to move in the afternoon of 2nd November, 1978. The Unit convoy had to move non-stop from Hyderabad to Chikmaglur, a distance of over eight hundred K.M.'s. The weary and fatigued drivers drove on stubbornly, stopping only to sprinkle water over the sleepy eyes and pouring cup after cup of hot tea down their throats, so that they did not just collapse over their steering wheels in sleep.

By the evening of the next day, I drove into Chikmaglur at the head of a small advance party. The town seemed to be eagerly awaiting our arrival. The very appearance of our convoy sent a flutter through many hearts. I drove straight to the S.P.'s office where the I.G.P. of the state was also present. To dispel any possible apprehensions that we had come to displace them, I made it absolutely clear that we had no such special instructions and had come only to assist them. The police chief, after my clarification, felt visibly relieved.

During this period, the news media displayed unprecedented interest in the induction of the C.R.P.F. For a number of days, we occupied prominent headlines in the national as well as the regional dailies. The progress of movement of the C.R.P.F. units towards Chikmagalur was reported with great gusto. Many political heavy-weights gave animated statements in the press for and against the deployment of the Force for the election.

Later in the night, Sh. S.B. Narayana Rao, Commandant of the Group Centre at Avadi who had been placed in temporary command of the 5th Battalion also joined me. Both of us discussed the ways and means of keeping our profile low and thus steer clear of all controversies in the media. This could be done by keeping ourselves aloof from the media so that they were not able to weave any unwanted stories around us. It was, indeed, a tough job to hide in the corners when the lime light followed us everywhere all through.

By 4th November, all the sub-units of the two battalions had occupied their assigned posts of deployment. Some of the companies had to cover another around two hundred K.M. to reach their places of duty. On 5th November, the polling opened on a brisk note, despite continual rain. About mid-day I had to rush to a polling booth in the main bazaar where some trouble had erupted. The very appearance of the C.R.P.F. calmed the things down. The voters and political volunteers assembled at the spot went hoarse shouting slogans like, 'We want C.R.P.' and 'C.R.P. Zindabad'. All this was music to our ears. It was, indeed a rare occasion when any of our officers could have dispersed the frenzied mobs with a mere wave of hand, accompanied by a smile.

The only assurance the crowd demanded was that our contingent shall remain present on the spot till the polling was over. This was done without any fuss. 'The Indian Express' issue of 6th November aptly recorded: "The C.R.P. deployed in the Chikmagalur Lok Sabha constituency have become popular over-night. Wherever they go on call of duty, they are greeted by the people like war heros` returning home triumphant. The C.R.P. presence, some voters confessed, had given them supreme confidence".

It was not only the Janata Party men who had welcomed the induction of the C.R.P. Force, but the Congress (I) elements also now seemed to be equally happy about it. All that the peaceful people of Chikmaglur wanted was peace and at this hour, words 'C.R.P.F.' and 'Peace' had become synonymous. The local authorities also lost no time in realizing that the C.R.P.F. was a highly effective and impartial force. They increasingly started placing confidence in us. Later, conceding a strongly voiced public demand, the job of guarding the ballot boxes and the counting arrangements were exclusively entrusted to us. The counting was smoothly completed by the morning of 8th November. The constituency elected Indira Gandhi as its representative.

With election fever over, Chikmaglur started breathing softly again. The C.R.P.F., however, continued to be in news for some more time. The discussion now was on the issue if the Force should have been called earlier than it was. The Karnataka opposition leader, Subbiah, expressed his view in the legislative assembly: "If only the C.R.P. had come early, Gaythri would have been saved. It was the C.R.P. which prevented a more serious blood-bath and rolling of more heads".

(A reproduction from the writer's article in the C.R.P.F. Newsletter and Magazine of 31.12.1978.)

30. GLOW OF WARMTH

Writer shown with Late Giani Zail Singh

He was not only a house-hold name in our town, Jaitu, but also everybody seemed to know him intimately. Even we as children were well aware about the police tortures he had undergone in the neighbouring state of Faridkot as a freedom-fighter. When the independence finally dawned over our sub-continent, many political sufferers of yesteryears found political prominence knocking at their doors. He took to politics as fish takes to water. Many years later his political acumen and numerous qualities of head and heart were to see him occupying the highest office of this land. I am, of course, talking about Giani Zail Singh.

This was the time when he was trying to get into the big league. He had already been a minister in the tiny state of Nabha and was now contesting for a berth in the P.E.P.S.U. (Patiala and East Punjab States Union) legislative assembly. He was sitting on a carpet before a small select gathering of the town in a local inn. We children were also around out of curiosity to see what the wazirs (ministers) looked like. The man in front of us looked plain and simple like a few who surrounded him. He could be taken for a teacher, a clerk, a preacher or just about anybody. Yet, there was a quiet dignity and some extra-ordinariness about him.

Incumbency in a democracy is generally a negative phenomenon for the rulers. It breeds exasperation, criticism and desire for change, as they often fail to meet the ever-rising common aspirations. The gathering on this occasion was no exception and they were duly critical about the performance of Giani ji during his ministerial stint. Despite this, it was decided in the end to extend him full support on the ground that at least the people could take him as their own man.I did not get another opportunity to see him during the next 28 years. During this period, he had rapidly risen in his political stature and was last the Chief Minister of Punjab. I then happened to be a commandant in the C.R.P. Force.

In 1978, the 51st battalion that I commanded was inducted in the Chikmagalur parliamentary constituency area in Karnataka. The sleepy town had suddenly shot in to prominence as the former Prime Minister, Indira Gandhi, had decided to contest for the parliamentary seat from this place. After ensuring that my men had occupied their assigned places of deployment to help in the smooth conduct of the election, I went to the local rest house to call on the two Union Home Ministers of State who were camping there. Since they were not around at that point of time I decided to wait.

Soon Giani ji emerged from his room and he was there was in front of me. As I paid him my compliments and reminded him of his election eve visit to my town, he took me in his arms warmly, without bothering a least that I was on duty and was in my uniform. After this we settled down on chairs in the ante chamber to give an update to each other as to what had gone with us during the last few decades. Nearly an hour went by. Since I had to run around to have a look at the security arrangements for the election, I sought his permission to leave. Giani ji, however, then seemed to have all the time in the world at hand. He insisted that I should stay for a while more. Finally when I again begged leave of him, he again hugged me affectionately and said that I should not hesitate to come to him, if ever I needed his help.

Come 1980, Indira Gandhi again bounced back to power. I then happened to be the establishment officer of my Force, having my office in the North Block. Gandhi ji was soon inducted in the Union Cabinet as Home Minister. Now, he had his high office just a floor above mine. However, my meeting him now for a minute to pay respects, proved to be such a wild goose chase that I finally dropped the idea.

However, after a few months, we assembled in the Vigyan Bhawan for the annual Commandant's conference. Giani ji was our honoured chief guest. I got a chance to meet him during the lunch interval. As soon as he was able to recall our meeting at Chickmagalur, he took my hand soulfully and held it close to his heart for good about five minutes, while we talked. Good old Giani ji had not changed even one bit over the highly eventful years that he had gone through.

(A reproduction from the writer's article in 'The Pioneer' on 18.9.1998.)

31. A TRUTH STRANGER THAN FICTION

There is always a flutter in the corridors of power when a new government is about to assume office. Specially, the bureaucratic glands get furiously at work to secrete the much needed adrenalin in preparation for the impending reshuffles. It is also time for some swollen heads to shrink to their normal size and for some individuals sulking in the shadows to suddenly emerge into the sunshine. This is an opportunity for some Chief Secretaries and Director's General of Police to shed their phony portfolios like 'Harijan Welfare', 'Police Housing' and even 'Civil Defence', 'Disaster Management' and 'Research and Training' and the like and to be appointed as the proper Chief Secretaries and Director's General.

Curiously, with the return of Indira Gandhi to power at New Delhi in 1980, even a poor constable of the C.R.P. Force had also to hastily pack his bags from the place, along with the complete line up of the seniors above him. This is how it all happened.

During my service with the central police organizations, I had the opportunity to come in contact with some impeccably honest officers. Late P.R. Rajgopal stands tallest among them in my mind. Honesty came naturally to him— never once did I see him making an exhibition of it. Sometime in mid 1979, he assumed charge as the Director General of the C.R.P. Force. At this point of time an officer of Commandant's rank acted as a sort of Establishment Officer to the Force. The appointment carried quite some clout as this functionary worked directly under the Director General, having his office in the Central Secretariat and dealt with matters connected with the career interests of the officers.

There were naturally quite a few aspirants for the job. I was then nearly among the junior most Commandants and many of my seniors had a service record decidedly superior to mine. Despite this, Mr. Rajgopal picked me for the post for some reason. I, thus, came to be suddenly seen as the blue-eyed boy of the Director General and my stock in Force shot up overnight. Accordingly, we moved to Delhi and set up our temporary home in a Swiss-cottage in our complex at the Ravindra Rangshalla, awaiting allotment of the proper government accommodation. I was permitted the customary privilege of having the personal staff of my choice. Among them was my old faithful constable Harender Nath Singh who later retired as a Sub-Inspector. Beset as he was with some family problems, the Delhi posting brought him considerable relief.

The mid-term polls to the Lok Sabha had just been announced. My father, a happily retired man, who had all the time in the world to have a look at the shadows of the coming events, once casually mentioned to Harender that his posting at Delhi depended on the outcome of the impending elections. The poor fellow looked quite lost, unable to understand how his posting was connected with the historic event. He thought my father was trying his hand at astrology. However, the seemingly prophetic words had just poured forth from a simple logic.

Mr. Rajgopal happened to be the former secretary to the Shah Commission. He sat in all grace close to Justice Shah, while Mrs Gandhi stood answering allegations. With her return to the Prime Ministerial chair, he could not hope to hold on to the high profile post of the Director General C.R.P.F. Along with the man had to perish all the persons considered close to him.

Mrs. Gandhi did return to power with a thumping majority. It was, however, not in her nature to chase her adversaries like a person possessed and thus, keep them in news all the time. She rather liked to just push them aside and leave them there to their fate. Accordingly, Rajgopal was just handed over his orders for repatriation to his parent cadre in the Madhya Pradesh Police and then forgotten about. But the self-respecting officer preferred putting up his papers for premature retirement and was allowed to retire in peace. I also duly got my marching orders. My regret, however, is that poor Harender also got kicked out of his posting.

How funny that his puny luck got entangled with that of the strongest Prime Minister of the country who in synchrony with the 'Iron Lady of England' (Mrs. Thatcher) was referred to as the 'Steel Authority of India'. But, then truth can sometimes be stranger than fiction.

(A reproduction from the writer's article in the "Hindustan Times' of 2.4.1998.)

32. HIDING HISTORY IN EYES

I never had any illusions of being a multi-faceted genius. I, nonetheless, always felt that I had lived a rather fascinating life, breathtaking in variety and adventure. After all, I have been a professional painter, a script-writer, a singer, an actor, an associate film director of sort, research scholar, a soldier, a cop, a magistrate, a commando, a freedom fighter and have now ended up as a freelance journalist, author and a lawyer. I had the privilege of putting on four uniforms in my career— the olive-green of the army, khaki of police, grey of a black-cat commando and the black of a lawyer.

I have been on friendly terms with a number of celebrities, including a President of the country and two Governors. I had an occasion to conduct Smt. Indira Gandhi around during the 2nd Asian Veterans' Athletic Meet. As a 12 year old, while leading a pack of much older boys, I managed to meet and talk to Nargis, one of the top film heroines of the time. In 1955, while still a minor I went to offer 'satyagrah' for the liberation of Goa when quite a few freedom fighters had already fallen to the Portuguese bullets and suffered terrible tortures at their hands.

All this, I thought, entitled me to believe that I had lived a life king-size. This was, of course, till I met my old faithful, Hari Bahadur, years back. This boyish faced Gurkha served as waiter in our officers' mess, while I was the second-in-command at the C.R.P. Force group centre at Delhi. A quarter of century had rolled by when I saw him again during the C.R.P.F. anniversary celebrations in 1998. While I had opted to retire prematurely, my erstwhile colleagues had meanwhile risen to the rank of inspectors' general of police, but poor Hari still continued to be a humble Group-D employee— sadly, there are no promotional avenues for our enrolled followers.

Handsome Hari of yester years still looked quite presentable. He seemed to enjoy his work and was our show-piece waiter for such occasions. There he was floating around deftly among the V.I.P. 's serving them with a smile and cheerful alacrity and making them feel welcome. He had located me with my family in the crowd and as soon as the V.I.P. 's departed he literally came flying towards us. We could feel the flutter in his heart. His warmth and humility set me thinking.

Here was a man who had made his mark in the job entrusted to him. He had the privilege of serving and having a close look at the facial contours of so many men of our destiny—— Presidents, Prime Ministers and a host of other high dignitaries. His innocent eyes preserved a good part of our history. Humble may have been his job profile, the cheerful man occupied an enviably high position on the happiness index.

He took us to the officers' mess complex which had since undergone a lot of refurbishing and looked all the more gorgeous. I suddenly remembered that the tele-serial 'Fauzi' was shot at this location and wondered where the now famous Shahrukh Khan (the hero of the serial) had stayed. Hari pointed to Room No. 6 (then numbered 3) and said the whole bunch of them had been lodged there, while Colonel Kapur (the producer / director) and his daughter (the heroine) were accommodated in the adjoining V.I.P. room. Once the super star had also borrowed Hari's uniform for a shot.

So, our Hari Bahadur's life had been no less eventful and fascinating than mine. All my illusions of extraordinariness thus crumbled in a heap before this humble man. I have, however, since learnt to enjoy my high status as a common man.

(A reproduction from the writer's article in the 'Hindustan Times' of 8.4.1999.)

33. DUTY IN DEFIANCE OF TEARS

By then I knew that he had lost his mother a few days back. But he happened to be an important member of our cultural troupe that was to perform on the C.R.P. Force Anniversary. I had thought of withdrawing him from the party and sending him on leave. I do not know why I held myself back. Perhaps I was curious to know what stuff my man was made of and how far he could push himself on the road to duty with a wounded heart.

Finally, it was time for the function and there he was on the stage. He sang while his heart wept. His melodious performance drew a prolonged applause from all, including myself, his commanding officer. While others just appreciated his singing talent, in me there was a surge of pride over something vastly more significant.

The function over, he, Gyaneshwar his name, was now an ordinary mortal in tears before me, with an application for leave in hand. When I asked him why he had not asked for leave earlier when his mother had died about a fortnight back, he simply said that he had been given a privileged job to do and for the purpose spared of the daily parade and other routine duties for about a month. So, he could not back out when it was time to perform. I sanctioned his leave straight away.

It was now for me to reward him suitably for his superlative sense of duty. I could have just awarded him a commendatory entry in his service records or granted him a small monetary reward in my competence. But this was something for which the other members of the troupe were also routinely due. He deserved something more substantial. I thought that it should be an out-of-turn promotion for him from the rank of a constable to a Naik.

There were, however, a few problems on the way. Although, as per the C.R.P. F. statute, I happened to be the appointing authority up to the rank of Inspector of police, most of our powers had come to be controlled by our Force headquarters. Too much of centralization normally results in administrative confusion, but in our case it was well-meant. The idea was to raise the level our men's cadre, so that the juniors in one unit did not go over their seniors in other units.

The implication of my decision was that I had to take the approval of my I.G.P. for its implementation. Fortunately, he was there with us in Nagaland shortly on our inspection. He readily approved my idea as I explained it to him. The second hitch was that his accelerated promotion could cause heartburn to his seniors, waiting for elevation near the top of the ladder. So, I collected the men in my unit durbar (Sainik sammelan) and apprised of them what I intended to do. I then asked them to raise hands, if they were happy over Gyaneshwar's instant promotion as Naik. All hands went up spontaneously and, to my relief, the first to go up was that of the jawan on top of the waiting list for promotion. This is the stuff our soldiers are made of.

Now, whenever a Sachin Tendulkar, rising above his personal grief, stands up manfully to do his duty by the nation, the face of Gyaneshwar flashes before my eyes.

(A reproduction from the writer's article in the 'Hindustan Times' on 10.9.1999.)

34. THE V.I.P. ROOMS AT BORJAR

In its own quiet way the C.R.P. Force has made a very significant contribution in keeping the country together. Wherever there is internal disturbance, these peace-keepers to the nation are always around. Since, over the years, our North-east has been a perpetual trouble spot, there has been a heavy deployment of the Force in the region all through.

21 Battalion of the Force was then located at Guwahati, the gateway to our North-east and I was the second-in-command of this unit. As a side job, we had to ensure that our top brass while on visit or in transit through the place got the facility of the V.I.P. rooms at the local Borjar airport. Only a handful of the high dignitaries and celebrities were entitled to the privilege of these rooms under the rules. Our I's. G. and D's. I.G. were by no means on this elite panel. Yet, it would be deemed a great administrative failure on our part, if we failed to secure this privilege for them. So, we had to use all our liaison skills like keeping the airport manager in good humour and also to resort a bit of 'dadagiri' for the purpose. I do not recall any of our senior officers ever having to miss the comfort of the V.I.P. longue. We somehow always managed it.

Unfortunately, on this occasion, both the V.I.P. rooms stood already booked — one for Late Mohammad Rafi, the celebrated playback singer and the other for an ambassador. Displaying the devil-may-care attitude, we lodged our I.G.P. in the ambassador's room. Finding the room occupied, the diplomat made himself comfortable in the adjoining room which stood booked for Rafi. Leaving his brief case there, he casually strolled out. After a while, Rafi and his entourage that included the sex siren of the times, Jayshree T, also arrived. We diverted him to the room occupied by the ambassador. When the ambassador saw all this commotion around his room, he rushed back. Taking him to be a curious fan, the toughies of the troupe tried to push him away. To save the situation, I had to yell at them that the gentleman should at least be allowed to pick up his brief case. To our relief, the ambassador did not create any further fuss once his brief case was handed over to him.

The flight was now ready for departure. Before the departure was announced to the general passengers, the airport manager escorted the V.I.P.'s to the aircraft. The I.G.P. was keen on taking along a note on the Bodo problem in the area which I had drafted for him at the last moment. By now our steno had finished the typing. I went to deliver the copy to the I.G.P. He was normally an exceptionally well speaker, but had a little tendency to stammer under excitement. To our embarrassment, he went in to his stammering mode while thanking me rather too profusely for the draft. Jayshree T was sitting close to him alright, but I do not think that his excitement really radiated from this source.

(A reproduction from the writer's article in 'The Tribune' of 27.7.2005.)

35. A SOLDIER STUNG INSIDE

My 37 Battalion, C.R.P. Force was then deployed for operations against the Naxalites in Srikakulam district of Andhra Pradesh. I held an important position in the unit. In the absence of the second-in-command, I, as the senior most deputy superintendent of police, officiated on this appointment. Our commandant, an easy-going Gurkha, had just come on deputation from the Orissa Military Police. He had very little knowledge of the C.R.P.F. working ethos. Besides, his interest level was also low, as he was on the verge of retirement. He somehow felt that the command of the unit could be safely outsourced to me and he could have a well-deserved rest at the fag end of his career. I was thus put in the position of a Marhatta Peshwa or a Japanese Shugen, as far as my unit was concerned, because the commandant was content to be just the titular head. This was, indeed, an undesirable situation, given rise to by the hurried expansion of the Force.

A platoon of the unit, under command of Sub-inspector Madhawan was placed at the village of Garudbhadra to guard a landlord who happened to be a prominent Naxalite target. Just after a few days a wireless message was received that a Naxalite 'dalam'(group), led by one Tamad Ganpati, had shot dead this man. My first reaction was to issue a nasty signal to Madhawan asking him to explain his failure to secure the man. However, my sense of discretion held me to back. I thought I must first visit the spot and hear the sub-inspector as to how this happened.

On reaching Garudbhadra I found the man in tears and cursing himself. In a typical south-Indian accent, he said between sobs, "Am ko to mar jana chahiye (I feel like killing myself). I have brought disgrace to the Force". I soon learnt that Madhawan could hardly be blamed for the mishap. The landlord had slipped away from his tightly guarded house by scaling his backyard wall to his farm, as he was worried about his standing crop. Ganpati got him there.

Thus, rather than condemning Madhawan, I ended up consoling the man who was feeling stung inside. He felt comforted when I told him that from then onward Tamad Ganpati was going to be his concern. He went after the offender like a man possessed. Every other day there were reports that the criminal had narrowly escaped at Madhawan's hands. Meanwhile our men apprehended and liquidated quite a few other Naxalites. The rest, including Ganapati, were put on the run.

Just after a couple of months, I was promoted and posted out. While leaving to join duties at my new place of posting I felt the satisfaction of, more or less, finishing with the Naxalite menace in the area. In fact, there was a long lull at the place after I left the district, though undoubtedly, something was still simmering there under the surface. Some of our politico-administrative weaknesses have since brought the problem back in a more virulent form.

As far as Tamad Ganpati is concerned, I soon learnt that he had been liquidated in an encounter. I do not know if it was Madhawan's men who accounted for him. I am also not sure if Madhawan is happy about it. After all he was a God-fearing individual having no personal animosity against anybody. He was just a humble peace-keeper to the nation, keen to do his duty well.

(A reproduction from the writer's article in 'The Tribune' of 29.8.2006.)

36. IN THE CORRIDORS OF POWER

There used to be a post of Assistant Director (Adm.), a sort of establishment officer of the Central Reserve Police Force, in the rank of a commandant. This functionary dealt with the appointment, promotions, postings, leave and confidential reports of the officer cadre in the Force. He was directly responsible to the Director General and had his office in the North block of the Central Secretariat. He acted as a sort of bridge between the Government and the Force. He was the only staff officer authorized to authenticate in the name of the President all the matters related to the Force after these met the Government approval. No wonder then that the post carried a clout far in excess of the rank of the appointee.

Late Mr. P.R. Rajgopal who was earlier the secretary to the Shah Commission (appointed to look into the alleged misuse of authority by the Indira Gandhi government) was posted as the Director General in the wake of a mini-mutiny in the C.R.P.F. in 1979. He had a great desire to restore the Force to its old glory. He, thus, went about visiting all his battalions deployed all over the country to carry a message that the recent turbulence needed to be forgotten quickly as a bad dream.

During his visit to my 13th Battalion at Kalyani in West Bengal, he noticed that the upheaval had not left even a minor scratch on my men. They seemed to be exuding a feeling of all being well with the world. The D.G. gave the credit for this soothing state of affairs to me, though, in all fairness, it should have largely gone to the excellent team work of my officers like Dhananjaiah, Puran Singh, Gaje Singh, Madusoodhanan and others. Anyway, the Director General felt that I could be of service to him in his mission. So, he appointed me to the high-profile post of the establishment officer of the Force over the head of many competent seniors. Thus, I had my first taste of being in the corridors of power in the Central Secretariat and felt good about it for a while.

Soon I found the officers coming to me in droves with all sorts of problems. Whenever, I was not able to help them I felt uncomfortable. Finally, I felt that there was hardly any fun involved in my position. In any case, with the return Mrs. Gandhi to power in early 1980, Mr.Rajgopal became a persona non grata. Along with him, not only

I but also my personal staff down to my office orderly got shunted from the Secretariat. Mr.Rajgopal applied for voluntary retirement. Mrs. Gandhi had the grace not to chase him the way she herself had been chased after losing power in 1977. He was allowed to retire and die in peace.

A few years later, I also sought early retirement to pursue my interests in some research work. My scholarly inclinations drove me soon to become a freelance journalist. Though I wrote on a wide variety of subjects ranging from international affairs to information technology, history and law emerged my principal areas of interest. So I went for post-graduation in history and a degree in law. While applying for admission to the LL.B. course, I had to appear in a pre-admission test. I was placed first in this competition and the then serving secretary of the parliamentary affairs stood second. Understandably, the serving secretary could not attend the evening classes on regular basis. He thus needed somebody to brief him about the daily lectures. This brought the two of us together as personal friends in course of time. He addressed me as 'sir' for being a year older and I always took care to return the compliment in view of his high station in life. In my case, I meant it and for him, it was just a matter of courtesy.

Often he would invite me to his office in the Parliament House and later in the Central Secretariat to discuss the lectures in the class or for proceeding together to the university campus for examinations. I thus found myself back in the corridors of power as a curious visitor. With no strings of responsibility attached to it this time, I enjoyed being there.

(A reproduction from the writer's article in 'The Tribune' of 24.10.2007)

37. THE RETURN OF THE REBELS

During my service in the armed forces I served as many as eight tenures in our North-East. In fact, that was the place where action was all these years. Every state of the region has its own identity and ethos. Among these, Nagaland fascinated me the most. Nagas are a brave, hardy and principled people. Nearly all of them have turned Christians under the influence of the Christian missionaries who had a free run in the area during the British regime.

During the active phase of the insurgency there, the armed forces suffered quite a few ambushes at their hands. But Nagas would never attack women and children. Being devout Christians, they would also not go for ambushes on Sundays. They were otherwise extremely daring. If any of us tried to act funny with their women, they would first put him on notice. Those who persisted on not taking their warning seriously often got liquidated in ambushes.

In 1972, I got posted in 36 Battalion, C.R.P. Force which happened to be deployed in the Chakesang region which was then the epicenter of insurgency in Nagaland. The unit was led by an excellent commanding officer, Indra Singh, who also followed the rules of the game like Nagas and was compassionate to the core. In a personally led operation, he captured a self-styled major general of the underground Naga army (we understandably referred to all functionaries of the underground Naga setup as self-styled) who was then placed well above Muivah and Isaac Swu, the surviving stalwarts of the rebel hierarchy today.

The prisoner was thoroughly interrogated, but never allowed to be ill-treated. In fact, our kind-hearted commandant gave his own quilt to him to make his stay in the prisoner's cell of our quarter guard comfortable. The Naga underground officials had a special fondness for issuing written orders. This often landed them in trouble with us and the courts. After a few months of the capture of the SS general, we were able to lay hands on one Punuro, a SS colonel in their setup. He had in his pocket a leave certificate signed by his superior who was none other than Issac Swu (then a SS brigadier). We immediately went after this high profile target, but Swu escaped from us by the skin of his teeth. I got posted out of the area soon after.

I returned to Nagaland four years later as the commanding officer of the 51 Battalion of my Force. The unit was then attached to an infantry brigade commanded by Brigadier A.K. Chatterjee who went on to become the G.O.C.-in-C of the Southern Command of the army during our operations in Srilankan. Muivah and Isaac Swu were then still around hiding in the jungles of Myanmar.

Quite a few important functionaries of the Naga underground outfit had, however, joined the national mainstream by now and settled down to a peaceful life. I contacted one such senior leaders and was able to persuade him to write a letter to Muivah to settle for peace. He and Swu, however, persisted with their rebellious ways for many more years. During these years, these rare survivors of the counter insurgency operations rose quite high in stature and have now been negotiating peace with the government for quite some time on tough terms. But once out of jungles, you rarely go back there. So, we, more or less, have been able to bid goodbye to insurgency in Nagaland for all practical purposes.

(A reproduction from the writer's article in 'The Tribune' of 13.9.2007.)

38. A CASE OF NATURAL JUSTICE

In 1973, I was commanding a detachment of three companies of the 21 Battalion, C.R.P. Force at Guwahati. One of these companies was stationed in the local police lines. The Superintendent of Police of the district was none other than K.P.S. Gill who was destined to go down in our police history as 'Super Cop' for rooting out terrorism from the soil of Punjab.

In the absence of the company commander, this sub-unit was in the temporary command of Inspector Bhanwar Singh. Liquor was then not easy to come by in the C.R.P.F. units deployed in peace areas. However, I, with my army background, always managed to get some for my detachment from the army sources. The company planned to have some celebration in its sub-ordinate officers' mess. So, I issued them a bottle of rum on their request.

After the party in the mess, Safai Karamchari Bhajan Singh was called there to clean up the place. An athletically built sub-inspector, Ram Singh, a participant in the function, lost his shirt for some reason over the diminutive Bhajan Singh and in a fit of rage, he administered a strong kick to him in the abdomen. The poor fellow fell on the ground clutching his abdomen.

He was immediately evacuated to the local Gauhati Medical College hospital. When an abdominal surgery on him confirmed that his intestines had been badly crushed, I suspended the sub-inspector. As it appeared that the case could be beyond my own judicial competence, I lodged a F.I.R. with the local police. After a few days his condition deteriorated and poor Bhajan Singh appeared to be visibly sinking. On my request, a local magistrate was deputed to record his dying declaration. Sadly, the man did not last long after that.

Law had to take its own course with S.I. Ram Singh. And we were in the same predicament that late Parween Mahajan's family must have felt recently. We did want the offender to be punished suitably, but after losing one brother we did not want to lose another. Anyway, Ram Singh soon got released on bail to come back to us. He was rightly not charged for murder in the absence of the intent to murder or even the knowledge that his kick would kill Bhajan Singh. The days went by. Ram Singh appeared hopeful that he would get out of all this with no or light punishment. We, on our part, did not want to go over board to have him punished adequately. We just left the things to flow on their natural course.

One day, there was a prominent news item in 'The Assam Tribune' that a body had been found in a drain close to the Malegaon stadium where Ram Singh`s company happened to be located. We deputed an officer to have a look at it because our Ram Singh had also been reported missing a day before that. However, before we could have a look at it, the body had been disposed of, though its hands were retained for finger-printing. We got these prints and had these compared with those of Ram Singh in the forensic laboratory at Shillong.

The comparison confirmed that the body was of our own sub-inspector. His murderer was nabbed with the help of the dog squad. He turned out to be a man punier than even late Bhajan Singh. Thus, the nature seemed to have gone rather in a Bollywood mode to deliver poetic justice in the case.

(A reproduction from the writer's article in 'The Tribune' of 15.1.2008.)

39. THE ETERNAL CYCLE

As you put on years, you see the generations disintegrating. First, you see your grandparents doing a disappearing act. You are then too young to understand the true significance of this phenomenon of earthly existence. When you grow older your parental generation starts vanishing, leaving you sad and disillusioned. This eternal procession of life, thus, keeps moving relentlessly forward into some shadowy unknown, leaving you wondering, if at all there is any purpose to life.

Recently, I happened to attend a get-together of our retired Central Reserve Police Force officers at Chandigarh. Nearly a generation back, we, as a sort of peace-keepers to the nation, were scattered all over the country— even at places as far removed as the Indira Point in the Andaman and Nicobar Islands, Ladakh and Lakshadweep etc. We had our footprints even in Europe, Africa, Srilanka and Latin America.

We dealt with dacoit gangs, insurgents, agitators, terrorist and, in fact, trouble-makers of all hues. In most of our wars and border skirmishes, we gave and drew first blood. All of us often took mortal risks in the line of our duty and few of us got martyred in the process. Some of us got decorations for our sacrifices and hard work and some remained unsung. We often had to suffer 'Murdabad' (Death to you) slogans from our own people for attempting to restore peace among them. This is something that our regular army also does not have to put up with.

Appearance-wise, some of us in our heyday could pass for as film heroes— straight, well-proportioned, radiant and handsome. Time had now taken its toll on us. We had, for sure, moved into the sunset of our lives. Some of us still look presentable. A few others looked weary and haggard. Gone was the youthful exuberance of yesteryears. Yet, my friends wore a look of warmth and contentment about them, an evidence of a life well spent.

While floating among them, I learnt that some of them were managing businesses and earning many times more than what they did during their service. Some were involved in social work with the zeal of a mission. Others, barring a few, were also not doing badly. They were enjoying their retired life to the hilt. They carried memories on which books could be written or feature films made.

Yet, it was a sad feeling to call to mind that some of us would ourselves be reduced to memories when we happened to meet next, especially when we all knew that even the memories had a limited life span.

Just when these disconsolate ideas were trying to creep into my mind, I noticed some young officers managing the party from behind the scene with great gusto and trying to make us feel good. It was a great feeling that they were now doing what we did decades back. In them, we saw our own lives in play-back mode. All that had happened in the meanwhile was that the eternal cycle of life had just moved a notch forward.

(A reproduction from the writer's article in 'The Tribune' on 29.1.2009.)

40. THE HUMAN FACE OF THE POLICE

I have served in the armed forces as well as the police and am proud of them both. If the armed forces defend our sovereignty, the police produce the precious wealth of peace. Yet our people think poorly of the police while they have high opinion about our armed forces. It would be interesting to know why the soldiers are seen as heroes and the policemen as villains.

The East India Company was understandably profit-oriented and keen to repatriate maximum money back home. They, nonetheless, had plenty of political power to play with. So, they went for a cheap policing system that revolved round the S.H.O.'s who were paid a pittance, but were otherwise vested with an awful amount of raw authority to overawe and oppress the natives in imperial interest. Thus, the past of our police raises quite some stink. Besides, their present day masters also have a vested interest in the outdated imperial model of police—they resent it only when they are at the wrong end of the stick. Left to themselves, our policemen would like to have a purely professional profile and earn the love and respect of the citizens that they fully deserve.

I commanded 51st Battalion of the Central Reserve Police Force deployed for election duties in Kashmir in 1977. The main contestants in the field were the Sheikh Abdulla's National conference and the Janata/ Awami Action Committee combine— the Congress was then licking the wounds of the parliamentary elections held earlier that year.

The National Conference and the Awami Action Committee, going by the appellations of 'Sher' and 'Bakra', had traditionally been at logger`s head with each other for years. It was this historic hostility that had come to a head in this election. The activists of from both sides would fly to each other`s throat on slightest of provocations.

At one point in Srinagar, I encountered a mob throwing stones at a residential building. Rather than resorting to force to disperse the miscreants, I got into their midst alone to know firsthand why they had chosen to pelt stones on the residents of that premises. The frenzied men were stunned by my gesture and opened their hearts before me. I then learnt that they were agitated over their suspicion that the residents of the building had abducted their child and were going to harm him.

I invited five of their representatives to come with me to search the house and assured them that if the boy was found held there, the guilty would be straight away arrested for being brought to book. After some hesitation, the occupants finally agreed to the search of their house by the representatives of the crowd in tow with me. The boy was not found in the premises. True to their word, the crowd leaders signaled their people to disperse. It was a delightful sight for me to see them dispersing peacefully without any use of force by us.

The rest of my time in the valley was devoted to treating the injured from both the warring parties. My jeep, with my doctor and his medical staff, soon came to be seen as an ambulance rather than a police vehicle.

I am sure many of my brother policemen routinely take such risks and do humanitarian work while keeping an eye on the law and order. They are very much human. Only the system they are required to work in is inhuman.

(A reproduction from the writer's article in 'The Tribune' on 9.7.2007.)

41. A THING OF BEAUTY

While feasting his eyes over nature's bounty, an ecstatic poet pours forth, "A thing of beauty is a joy forever". These comely blossoms kept flashing back on his mind all his life to be "bliss of his solitude". Beauty of any sort has a mesmerising effect on our minds. Our doctrine of "Satyam, Shivam, Sundram" also takes due note of this phenomenon.

Human female is very much a part of this pageant of nature. She has been provided a face and figure that are matched only by the poetry, paintings and sculptures that these have inspired over the ages. This truth was quietly brought home to me when we went after some suspected Naxalite insurgents in a small village of Srikakulam district in Andhra Pradesh way back in 1969.

I was then officiating as the second-in-command of a C.R.P. Force unit deployed in the area. An anonymous letter was received at our headquarters naming three villagers involved with the extremists. We could not place much reliance on this information. Yet, we could not ignore it either. So, I marched to the village at the head of a company.

The villagers were asked to assemble at one place. They readily complied. I told the gathering that we had come looking for some suspects. When nobody responded to the three names disclosed by me, search parties were sent to get hold of any villagers who might have chosen to be in hiding.

After a while, Sub-Inspector Virender Singh, appeared with a young lady in tow. There was an air of innocence and freshness about her. She was by no means an unworldly beauty. Still, with the likes of her around, one felt good without even knowing the reason.

She innocently pointed to her husband in the gathering before me. This man happened to be one of the three that we were looking for. By trying to hide himself in the crowd the man had invited some more suspicion on himself. So, I decided to take him along for interrogation. This sent a wave of shock among the villagers. His handicapped grandmother crawled to my feet begging that no harm should come to him. The lovely lady, his wife, now looked deeply embarrassed at the turn of events.

In the end, the village elders undertook to produce all the three suspects before us for verification the next day. Thus, I agreed not to take him with us right then.

Before, however, we could turn our back, I got a glimpse of Virender Singh confronting the man just spared by us. The S.I. warned him in all seriousness that if he beat his young wife for giving him out, he would be back to give him hell. Our Virender was a happily married man and a well-intentioned person. Still the beauty of the lady seemed to have worked its own magic on him in some way.

As for me, I also took note of her. But, the nature and society had been kind enough to accommodate my very first choice in the matter of marriage. Thus, I always felt that my eyes had lost all their right to rove long time back.

(A reproduction from the writer's article in 'The Tribune' on 22.12.2008.)

42. AN AGE OLD ILLUSION

By now I am quite sure that all of us live under an illusion that we look much younger than what our actual age suggests. How young we really wish to feel depends on the magnitude of the mirage that we are in. At the base of this thinking is the man's futile quest for immortality which is really the privilege of just one being, God, and none else. Yet, the fact of life is that none of us wish to grow old or are ever ready to call it a day. In relation to these inevitabilities, we feel that it is yet too early. This is how the immortal lines of the Urdu poet, "Abhi to maen jawan hoon" (Presently, at least I am young), though having the definite pathetic overtones, ring so sweet to us.

All this notwithstanding, we still keep hearing the warning bells deep inside. Whatever arguments we may keep putting across to ourselves, we know the years would not ever stop rolling by ourselves. The struggle for age resistance is not only fought within our minds, the more nervous of us try to involve others in the game. Such people designedly throw a feeler around that age after all has caught up with them. What they expect to hear in return is an assurance that they still look youthful and had miles to go. The great misunderstanding thus remains permanently lodged in human psyche.

I have a first-hand experience to narrate in this regard. It happened when I was serving as a commandant in the Central

Reserve Police Force and had just landed at Mount Abu for some guest lectures at the Internal Security Academy there. J.S.Negi, a 'numbari' of mine in the Force (Numbaris, in Gorkha parlance, stands for the two soldiers assigned adjacent seniority in the force) was already there at the station. Negi was originally placed a notch below me. But he, on the strength of his abilities, as reckoned in our Force, had gone over me in seniority.

Numbaris, as we were, we suddenly happened to have toothache together almost out of nothing. Fortunately a visiting doctor was available in the local hospital on that day. We carried quite a bit of clout at the small place. So, there was no difficulty in fixing an appointment with him. The dentist was otherwise also an amiable and easy-going person. As he was about to fill up the age column on my admission slip, he did not bother to ask me about my age. He just had a fleeting look at my face, contorted out of nervous pain, and filled my age as 45. I was then around 42 and innocently believed that I looked to be in mid-thirties.

Therefore, the figure '45' against my name in the doctor`s form made my toothache feel a lot more severe. However, I felt a little relief when the same uneasy figure appeared on the form of Negi who, otherwise, happened to be good three years younger to me.

On our way back to the Academy, we fell completely silent and nearly forgot that we ever had a toothache. Some bigger psychological ache seemed to have taken its place. Now only one agonizing thought occupied our mind. How the doctor had placed our age even higher than our actual age. Were we the cases of undue wear and tear? Just when I was trying to console myself that the doctor might have estimated us to be older because of the senior rank that we held or there might even be something wrong with his eye-sight, my simple-minded friend from the Garhwal Hills suddenly broke his silence. My jaw fell further when he tried to make out that there was nothing much wrong with the doctor over-estimating my age, but doing so in his case was absolutely a blasphemy.

(A reproduction from the writer's article in 'The Pioneer' of 30.3.2000.)

43. THE FIRST FEMALE COMBAT UNIT OF THE COUNTRY

The 88th Mahila Battalion of the C.R.P. Force

They are symbolic of the women power of the nation. Raised in 1986, the 88th Mahila Battalion, C.R.P. Force, the first female combat unit of the country, is steadily building up a notable past. Their operational role is to tackle law and order situations involving women, searching and frisking of women, security of women's enclosures., guarding of vital areas less vulnerable from security angle and relief and rescue operations during communal holocausts and natural calamities. The unit has seen active service in the insurgency ridden states of Jammu and Kashmir, Punjab and many other disturbed pockets all over the country and even abroad. The unit opened its account of battle honours with a Sena Medal in Sri Lanka in 1988 and later went on to cover itself with glory by winning the coveted Ashok Chakra also, the highest peace-time gallantry award.

On August 12, 1988, the 'A' company of this Mahila battalion was airlifted to Sri Lanka as part of the Indian Peace-keeping Force. The sub-unit made its presence felt within days of its induction. Lance Naik Bimla Devi, the first woman recipient of a Sena Medal recalls how on August 31 at about 0830 hours, she was able to lay her hands on a L.T.T.E. militant, Kadita Uma, who had 1192 deadly detonators wrapped round her body. Her interrogation led the rounding up of a number of militants. Thus, a dangerous plot to sabotage and kill in the Elephant Pass area was pre-empted.

L/Naik Bimla Devi receiving Sena Medal from the Army Chief

In 1992, two sub-units of this battalion were deployed for active operational duties in the Srinagar valley and one each at Guwahati and Ajodhya. They regularly accompanied the Army/ C.R.P.F. raiding columns to flush out the Pakistan trained militants in J&K and the U.L.F.A. insurgents in Assam. The brave girls had to their credit the capture of 11 hardcore Hizbul Muzahideen militants, 16 A.K.47 rifles, 3 pistols/revolvers, four grenades and large quantity of other arms and ammunition. Fourteen of them got decorated with the commendation discs by the Chief of the Army Staff and the Director General C.R.P. Force. However, paths of glory sometimes lead to the grave and those who live by the sword have to die by the sword. The unit personnel have been subjected to a number of grenade/ mortar attacks and bursts from machine guns.

Ajai Raj Sharma, the then I.G.P.(Hqs) and a senior formation commander of the ladies outfit claimed that his girls were performing well beyond the expectations and with a great sense of purpose and pride. They were raised to deal with women agitators but very often they were up against the male trouble-makers also. There is, therefore, a special emphasis on unarmed combat in their training. A large number of judo awards won by the unit girls at national level are a testimony to their prowess in this area. These judo tigresses are, indeed a feared lot. Their battle-worthiness is well established by now. A need for expanding the female element of the Force began to be felt quite early and this has since been carried out. In fact, it was immediately decided in principle to add a platoon of female constabulary in every Rapid Action Force unit.

Attitudinally, these girls are highly competitive and courageous. Miss Amrit Brar, a directly appointed assistant commandant of the Mahila unit insisted on serving in a regular C.R.P.F. Battalion on her passing out in 1990. Later, as a commander of the special commando team in Srinagar, she discarded her bullet-proofs simply because the matching protection could not be provided to all members of her team. A brighter example of female prowess and chivalry in reverse flow is difficult to find. In fact, this would remind one of Babar refusing to get into a cosy cave on an atrociously chilly evening in Afghanistan, just because it was not big enough to shelter his men along with him.

It is operationally imperative that the ladies battalion maintains its young profile. With the authorized strength of 1151 personnel, including the clerical staff and hospital staff, the unit already had 270 married women, 168 of them happened to be mothers and 55 personnel remained on maternity leave on the average. In this scenario, the only thing that can help to maintain the youthful ethos of the unit to some extent is that 35 to 40 girls seek discharge every year, mostly on getting married. Perhaps some more steps are necessary to maintain the youthful character of the unit. For instance, their recruitment age could be reduced to a span of 17 to 21 years and they could be provided the facility of voluntary retirement from service after fifteen years of service.

The personnel of the Mahila Battalion do face some problems like the paucity of married accommodation, over deployment and the usual fall outs of hectic movement and uncertainties of tenure at a place. But they seem to be taking all this in their stride. Their then Dy. I.G.P., A.K.Bandopadhyay, disclosed that on the occasion of the visit of the Prime Minister, Late Rajiv Gandhi, in 1987, most of the unit girls insisted on doing the difficult obstacle course exercises like the vertical rope-climbing and monkey crawl etc. Many of them got bruised while at it, but their spirits remained high. They had a point to prove that they were not the push-overs.

(A reproduction from the writer's article in 'The Hindustan Times' of 28-6-1992.

44. THE OBVIOUS NEED FOR A THIRD FORCE

The law and order situation in the country has undergone a sea change over the years and there is an urgent need for a specialized force, other than the army and police, to meet the new situation. The suggestion is not to raise another paramilitary force, but to bind together the already strong paramilitary muscle of the country under a unified command to obtain maximum synergy. The 'Third Force', so constituted should have a proper Constitutional identity, a well-defined responsibility profile, adequate authority and resources at its direct command.

Over the years, the term security has come to acquire a new meaning. Earlier, the police force almost entirely concentrated on controlling crime. Hunting dacoits or chasing lightly armed revolutionaries or the unarmed agitators for freedom was then considered to be the most challenging aspect of their duties. The police did handle many civil disturbances during the pre-independence period, but the agitators were, by and large believers in non-violence and peaceful in their protest. So, public order was a subsidiary job for the police.

In such a situation, the police force of the country was quite capable of maintaining peace and order in the country without any undue strain on its nerves. In more serious civil disturbances, the district magistrates could always summon military assistance to provide support to the police. No neighbouring foreign power could then think in terms of administering 'thousand cuts' on the country.

The contours of our internal security have changed substantially since those days, but the systems and infra-structure to deal with it continues to be largely the same. The only perceptible changes that have taken place are the separation of the judiciary and executive, delinking of police from prosecution and removal of the provisions for martial law from our statute. All these reforms are laudable from the human rights angle, but it has not been easy for the peace-keepers to carry the burden of these ideals.

At this point, it is necessary to briefly examine the complexities that have crept into the law and order environment of the country. The most important aspect is the lopsided awakening that has come about. While the people have generally become aware of their rights, they continue to be largely ignorant about their duties. Bulk of the fear for the law is gone without being replaced by the respect for the law.

Secondly, there has been rapid criminalization of politics and politicization of police. Thirdly, religion which even earlier was a highly emotive issue has now acquired a highly fissionable character in the hands of the vote-hungry politicians. Finally, our nation seems to be facing a crisis of character. Even our well-intentioned leaders are obliged to waste bulk of their valuable time in totally unproductive political manoeuvres just to stay in power. So, even though we are still valiantly struggling to maintain our democratic system, the controlling of crowds and criminals in such a situation is a real tough job.

This is not to say that the army or police are no longer relevant or they have been found wanting in the performance of their duties. The two forces have been performing their assigned duties with a sense of purpose and pride. Yet, we have to face the fact that they are not the proper answer to the security situation that we have somehow landed into. Clearly, the baton and the bullet alone are not enough to deal with our present predicament. One has been created for the criminal and the other for the enemy. We really need a force having understanding of the rising aspirations of the people and yet uncorrupted by the local influences. It must have a truly nationalistic outlook and image, consistency of approach and plenty of staying power. It may occasionally incur wrath at regional level, but should enjoy the respect and confidence of the nation as a whole. It should be able to sustain our political will to stay together.

Our law does provide for the use of the armed forces for aid to the civil authority (Sections 131 &132 Cr.P.C.). They can be summoned for help in emergencies. However, it must be remembered that they are the ultimate weapon and therefore, cannot afford to fail even once. Routine deployment and over-exposure can make even the most elite force look ordinary. Our defence forces have very vast territory and economic interests to protect. They are the pride of the country and nothing should be done to put their shine at stake. Moreover, the army does have the strength of arms but not the proper attitudes to deal with civil disorders. A comparative study of our Army operation, 'Blue Star' and the National Security Guard operation, 'Black Thunder II', though mounted in somewhat different settings, would nonetheless prove this point fairly adequately.

If it is hazardous to use the army as police, it is equally short-sighted to use the police force in the role of army. During the problem of terrorism in Punjab, the Punjab Police was armed to the teeth to face the militants. When peace returned to Punjab by the Grace of God and Gill, did the police force quickly return to its old ways of work all that easily? The automatic rifles, carbines and mortars can be withdrawn without fuss, but attitudes acquired during the anti-militancy operations take ages to get erased from the minds. For a long while the ordinary offenders might be seen and get treated as terrorists. Otherwise also, a police force can never be expected to deal with a situation of covert war, having international ramifications, on a sustained basis.

Fortunately, the country has a strong paramilitary muscle already. The paramilitary forces, particularly the Central Reserve Police Force, have done their bit to keep the country together so far in the face of the fissiparous tendencies raising their ugly head here and there. But under the existing scheme of things, they can be inducted in the states only with their consent. Even when the states concur, they are obliged to work under the directions of the state officials. This lack of operational independence not only handicaps their initiative but also hurts their sense of purpose and pride.

New paramilitary forces have been mushrooming year after year and government after government. When we got independence we had had just one battalion of the Crown Representative's (Viceroy's) Police, later rechristened as the Central Reserve Police. Today, the C.R.P. Force itself is over two hundred battalion strong. By their side, have cropped up the forces like the Border Security Force, Indo-Tibetan Border Police, Central Industrial Security Force, Coast Guard, Special Frontier Force, National Security Guard, Special Protection Group, Rashtriya Rifles and others. If the idea is to out-people the people with police, this aim is just not achievable. It is a pity that while the paramilitary forces have proliferated purposelessly, cutting in to the role of one another, nobody has thought of giving them some Constitutional identity.

The answer to the problem is to let the army and police do their basic work. Militancy in its various forms— insurgency, terrorism and Naxalism etc, should not be confused with law and order. 'Police' and 'Public Order' are the state subjects and these could stay with the states. What happened in Punjab the other day and what is happening in the Jammu and Kashmir, North-East and the

Naxalism affected districts of many states is not a problem of law and order, but a situation of covert war. It should be understood as such.

The task of dealing with such serious internal disturbances should be handed over to a 'third force', constituted by merging the existing paramilitary forces. This force could be designated as the 'National Security Force' and headed by an officer of the rank of the Service Chiefs. It should have its tentacles throughout the length and breadth of the country. It should have the following corps under its command— Internal Security Corps, Border Security Corps, Industrial Security Corps and the Special Tasks Corps. The force should have proper intelligence cover and the authority to investigate matters falling in the domain of national security.

If somebody thinks that the new outfit would be unwieldy, he could be reminded that the defence forces are capable of fighting battles up to the level of a 'field army', which consists of around two and a half million soldiers. The proposed National Security Force could also thus be expected to be able to manage its half a million or so combatants adequately well.

There should be no Constitutional hurdle on the way of its raising either. After all, police power is the inherent power of every state. Besides, Article 355 (that casts a responsibility to protect the states on the Centre and consequently, the necessary authority for the purpose) and Entry 97 of List I of the Seventh Schedule (relating to residuary powers) of the Constitution, could provide the necessary legal locus to the Centre to raise such a force, without seeking any Constitutional amendment

(A reproduction from the writer's article in 'The Economic Times' of 11.10.1992)

(D) NATIONAL SECURITY GUARD

(The Black Cat Commandos)

Designed to descend on enemies like a bolt from the blue.

45. INDIA'S RESPONSE TO 26/11

The 'Black Cats' prove themselves yet again at the Taj Hotel at Mumbai

Pakistan has been for long working on its policy of delivering 'Thousand Cuts' to India. The unkindest of these cuts was inflicted in Mumbai on 26 November 2008. The gruesome 26/11 assault called for a strong action from our side. That the perpetrators could commit such a ghastly crime on our soil, makes it clear that Pakistan still considers India as a soft state. Many of us, in our anguish and anger, would have wished that our government should have responded in a similar manner as the Americans did following the 9/11 terrorist attacks.

But then India is not America. The USA happens to be the lone superpower of the world in terms of economic, technological and military strength. Besides, the country stands protected on its flanks by the two widest oceans of the earth, and has the benefit of weak neighbours to its north and south. Our situation is entirely different from theirs. We are still a developing economy and are vulnerable from all sides and on many other counts. We, thus, had to act differently within our limitations. Nonetheless, our response had to be adequate.

This is precisely what we have done. Firstly, the gallant men of our security forces, both from the Maharashtra Police and the National Security Guard, liquidated nine of the 10 attackers on the spot; and were able to capture the remaining one alive. Secondly, the captured assailant was dealt with strictly according to law with admirable amount of patience, giving him all opportunity to defend himself. He was hanged at the gallows as per his sentence, without bothering for any pressure from any side.

Now that all the 10 assailants have been sent packing to hell, a clear message must have gone to the terrorists that anybody intruding into our land for mayhem should be prepared to meet a certain death. The psychological impact of this implication is not going to get lost on them in a hurry. Thirdly, Pakistan itself has been brought under considerable pressure to deal with the handlers of the criminal adventure in its own backyard appropriately. The international community has stood firmly behind us while all this happened. This may be because some Americans and Jews also got killed in the crime. Terrorists do not mind spilling any blood. So long it is human, they are happy.

Unfortunately, far too many riff raff elements, wandering for bread and work, are at hand in this part of the world. Any number of Kasabs and Ismails can be picked up and brainwashed to kill the 'infidels' who are unprepared to believe that Prophet Muhammad is the only channel of communication between Allah and 'adami', or that the beautiful vale of Kashmir rightfully belongs to Pakistan. All that is needed for the purpose is an assurance of some money for their kin, a few helpings of mutton curry and the promise that, on their death, they would find 72 heavenly damsels lined up for them.

Some subjectivity might have crept into our initial response to the 26/11 tragedy. In the end, however, India has reacted well to the grim situation.

I may well be wrong, but from my assessment of the misadventure of 26/11, it appears to me that:- (a) Perhaps the elected government of Pakistan is not directly involved in this hideous crime. (b) Some non-state elements and also the state actors, not in control of the government, are very much a party to the outrage.(c) There is lately some realisation in Pakistan that terrorism is an ill-wind that does nobody any good. Over the last few years, the terrorist outfits have become a source of headache to the government as well as the people of Pakistan. Pakistan Army, however, has still not stopped dabbling with the idea that the terrorists are their strategic assets. (d) One reason for many troubles of Pakistan is that the Muslims have been led to believe that their religion is superior to that of others.

Until now we have been expressing anger against Pakistan as a whole, and squarely criticising its government for import of terror into our land and the rest of the world. Perhaps there is a need to re-orient our policy towards our western neighbour, keeping the above premises in mind. For instance, we have to, in some way, strengthen the hands of the elected government of Pakistan, so that the civilian setup there is able to put their lawless non-state actors as well as the recalcitrant state actors, especially their over-sized army, in control.

The people of Pakistan have no animosity towards India. Rather they subscribe to the view that we are their closest kin in terms of a shared history, ethnicity, culture and language, etc. The two countries are, after all, the joint winners of the most glorious war against imperialism in human history. Thus, once the Pakistan government starts reflecting the will of the people and acquires the capacity to implement it, most of the problems of the subcontinent would vanish.

The terrorist might appear to be a Frankenstein let loose by the Pakistan state, but today it is very much a victim of its own doing. The two nations now need to come together to put this jinn back into the bottle. Both sides have to appreciate the situational compulsions of each other. The need of the moment is to reduce trust deficit between us. Meanwhile we must be prepared to deter terrorists, the way we have done in this case, if Pakistan persists on delivering some more cuts on us.

(A reproduction from the writer's article in the 'Daily Post' on 28.11.20.)

46. THE MONALISA SMILE

During the closing phase of my career in the armed forces, I was deputed to assist in the raising process of an elite commando outfit, the National Security Guard. Even before this force became operationally functional, somebody in our media gave it the name 'The Black Cat Commandos'. The name has stuck to it since, though the late prime Minister, Rajiv Gandhi preferred to call the Force as 'The Black Panthers'.

After the organizational framework had been finalized, I found myself entrusted with the land acquisition work. What followed next was the scores of trips to various revenue offices, a plethora of correspondence and extensive leg-work. Some spirited and sustained hard work by the revenue officials, from the deputy commissioners down to the patwari's, made us the proud owners of over eighteen hundred acres of our land in Manesar and Smalkha in record time. In the bargain, I also got the reputation of being a great expert in all matters related to land, and collected quite a few friends in the revenue circles of Gurgaon and Delhi, besides in the public works departments and Delhi Development Authority.

Incidentally, our land at Manesar happened to have an earthen dam on one side. That put us in doubt at the last moment that the land that we were acquiring might be a water logged area. This took me to the irrigation authorities to know why this 'bandh' had to be put up in the first place. They showed me the original proposal papers for this project signed by the Executive Engineer, Lahore around one and a quarter century back! They also assured me that area does not have any history of water logging for the last at least one hundred years.

One day, I had a personal request from my Director General, Mr. Nagrani, who was in a bit of bother. He told me that he had set his heart on a few additions and alterations to his house in Vasant Vihar and he had duly submitted a plan for this to the Delhi Development Authority, meeting all their requirements. While he was patiently waiting for the sanction of his plan, he was given to understand by a worldly-wise friend that the D.D.A. would not clear his proposal, unless he agreed to part with some money. The D.G. loathed the very idea of paying bribes. But that plainly meant that he had to just forget about the planned additions and alterations to his house for ever.

He, however, knew that I had made some twenty-five trips to the D.D.A. to push one of our land acquisition files stuck with them. So, he thought of trying the one last time through me, before dropping the idea of renovating his house as a bad job. I had always found him a suave and refined individual and he had been particularly nice to me. It was, therefore, a pleasure for me to be of some help to him. I asked for the case file and went through it carefully. All the requirements of the rules seemed to have been met already.

On enquiry, I found that the matter was to be settled at the level of a particular director of the D.D.A. I knew this official to be a sincere and sober person and it was difficult for me to believe that he was part of the goings-on in the D.D.A. So I met him and, in the point blank manner of a soldier, apprised him of what our D.G. had been told about the state of affairs in his organization. I expected him to lose shirt and protest noisily over my suggestion that his was the most corrupt establishment. I also thought that he would shoot back at me the names of the departments that, in his opinion, were more corrupt than his own.

However, nothing of this nature followed. Instead, the gentleman permitted himself a faint smile, asked for the case file, had a quiet look at it and signed the sanction papers without any fuss. All this left me wondering what his smile was about. Some twenty-five years have since gone by. Yet, I have not been able to decipher that mysterious Monalisan smile.

(A reproduction from the writer's article in 'The Hindustan Times' of 27.9.1997)

2

THE POLICE ETHOS

They produce the precious wealth of peace

An oath hard to keep

47. THE PROBLEM OF POLICE IMAGE

Peace and orderliness have been the most valuable assets of the mankind ever since the dawn of civilization. When danger is around civilizations stop growing and cultures get pushed to the corners. Yet, the people, when they sleep in peace, tend to forget all about those who are awake for them. Sadly, in our part of the world a policeman is seen with fear in one eye and hate in the other. He is considered to be a dehumanized being, who believes only in boot and baton.

Not that the police third-degree is exclusively an Indian phenomena. It is an ugly fact of life throughout the world. There is no legal sanction for this brutality anywhere in the world. Yet, it persists as an essential tool of investigation because the viable alternatives for controlling crime are very few. Thus, lot of kicking and canning goes on in the confines of the lock-ups and interrogation rooms to thrash out information for prosecution. In fact, the human bodies are tormented in variety of many other blood-curdling ways also. In one case, a political detainee had his pajama ends tied near the ankles and a few mice were let in from above before the waist cord was tied. The man writhed in agony and irritation whole the night through. Another victim had a lighted hurricane lantern, without the cap, tied to his penis, with the tormentors controlling the flame according to the heat intended to be conveyed to his private parts.

Citizens are always willing to look the other way, if such treatment is reserved only for the hardened criminals. The trouble arises when some innocents also get sucked into the interrogation chambers as suspects. There is really no practicable way of avoiding it and no society has a proper answer to it. Hence the pernicious practice cannot be totally uprooted. For this the forensics would have to develop at a much quicker pace. Even then some physical coercion would be necessary to stop an accused being evasive with the police. However, the saddest part of it is that the third degree is not only resorted to for lifting the veil over the face of crime, but also to keep the critics of the rulers in fear of them.

In the Western fraternities, the police, undoubtedly, enjoy a much better image. However, this is only because they always behave nicely with the man in street. Otherwise, they act equally tough with the offenders. One may recall how Rodney King was accidently caught on video being beaten in to pulp by the U.S. police. Our god-man, late Bhagwan Rajnish who spent a few days in an American lock-up also did not have to say many nice things about the police there. In October, 1989, the British press broke the awkward news that some alleged I.R.A. activists who were subjected to intense third degree and were noticed being moved about nude in icy weather conditions, were finally found to be totally innocent. An Amnesty International report documents how brutally the refugees and asylum seekers are treated in Germany.

Unfortunately, we have been bequeathed a rather brutal police system created by the British to cater to their own colonial needs. It served them well, but it is now totally out of tune with our democratic order. Despite the fact that many of those who came to hold the reins of the country after our Independence had suffered terribly at the hands of this boorish outfit, they appeared to be in no particular hurry to do something about its image and attitudes. They knew fully well that back home the British had an entirely different police structure, that not only commanded the confidence but also the love and respect of their countrymen.

In fact, the euphoria over our Independence evaporated much before the police reforms could be taken in hand. The power-seekers opened many fronts to reach the seats of power. With the running battles over regional, religious and host of other issues becoming the order of the day, all the imperatives of the imperial days returned even in more uglier form. The police came to be seen as the political prerogative of the ruling party to keep themselves in power and for settling scores with their political opponents.

The colonial police structure was built around the officers-in-charge of police stations who were often designated as the Station House Officers. This low-paid functionary (generally placed in the pay-scale of a upper division clerk) was loaded with an awful amount of raw authority over the natives. This served a dual purpose. First, an official of this level would never think big and secondly, this ensured cheap policing. The S.H.O. still constitutes the cutting edge in our police setup. His post at some places has been slightly upgraded to the rank of Inspector, which is still a subordinate (Group 'C') position. With his poor pay and bureaucratic status on one hand and the awful amount of authority thrust on him on the other, he continues to be highly susceptible to multi-pronged pressures. In fact, a political party coming to power first thinks of placing the S.H.O.`s of its choice in the police stations to get even with the former rulers, at whose hands it had suffered while in opposition.

In fact, our policeman also, in turn, carries an intense feeling of grievance against the society. Our law presumes him to be a liar—any confessional statement given by the accused to him or while in his custody, is not admissible as evidence in court, except for some limited purposes (Sections 25 to 27 of the Indian Evidence Act, 1872). Courts snub him day in and out. His pay packet and perks match poorly with the responsibility assigned to him and the status he is expected to maintain— just call to mind the oddity involved in the Bollywood producers portraying their Police Inspectors to be living in palatial bungalows. All this conveys an impression, as if it is believed that he, after all, has all the opportunity to supplement his income through 'hafta`s' and bribery.

The public, at best, regards a policeman as a necessary evil. There is really very little appreciation that he is not an unproductive segment of the society— he produces the precious wealth of peace. He often dies in the cause of his duty unwept, unsung and inadequately honoured. The highest honour that he is entitled to is the Presidents Police Medal for Gallantry which ranks woefully low on the warrant of precedence for the state awards.

In fact, the police is an area crying for reforms. If the police attitudes are to be improved action shall have to be taken on many fronts. The first and most important step in this direction would be to arrest the rapid politicization of police. The report of the Dharamvira Police Commission contains some valuable suggestions in this regard. Unfortunately, this document of national importance, to which a high-profile ex-director general of C.R.P. Force, N.S. Saksena, made a significant contribution, has been getting tossed about between the Centre and the states like a hot potato for decades and is even now gathering dust somewhere.

A few years back, some public spirited people like Padmashri Parkash Singh, the former director general of the B.S.F. and H.D. Shourie, the Director, Common Cause, took the matter related to the police reforms to the Supreme Court through advocate Prashant Bhushan, now a leading civil society activist. This resulted in some directions from the apex court. Even these do not seem to have been implemented in the right earnest. It appears that the existing police system is, in fact, quite to the liking of our politicians. They raise a hue and cry only when they are at the wrong end of the police stick.

The primary role of police is to ensure that the strong do not overawe and oppress the weak. This is the area where the citizens want their policeman to deliver. If he, instead, allows himself to become an instrument of awe in the hands of the high and mighty, he would never be able to inspire love and respect of the people. He would rather continue to radiate a feeling in public mind: "Na teri dosti achhi, na dushmani achhi" (One must treat friendship as well as enmity with police like plague).

(A reproduction from the writer's article in 'The Hindustan Times' of 14.1.1997.)

48. POLICING THE POLICE

I happened to be in London for about five weeks sometimes in 1989. During the second week of my stay there, a girl lodged a F.I.R. with the local police that the night before she had been raped by a police constable in his patrol car. The ghastly killing of two innocent men by the trigger-happy policemen in our capital in 1997 brought back to my mind the memories of the London incident.

The British have been our masters and still live as a role-model in our psyche. If there is something wrong over there, our own inequities tend to lose some of their stink in our mind. Thus, the incident of rape by the London bobby, though certainly nauseating, did not fail to give me a curious sense of comfort. So, crime within the police cadres was not an Indian phenomenon alone. I felt something like, "Dil khush hua masjid-e-viran ko dekh ke, meri tarah Khuda ka bhi khana kharab hai" (The desolate look of the mosque strangely gladdened my heart. After all, very much like my own situation, God`s abode is also not in all that happy position).

I had followed this case with great interest and curiosity. The investigations were initiated immediately and the accused cop charge-sheeted in a matter of days. The facts of the case, as brought before the trial court, were as follows: One fateful night the prosecutrix and her boyfriend came out of a pub after a long session of drinks around midnight. They were looking for some conveyance to go home when the accused, on beat duty in his patrol car, drove up to them. After routine questioning, he offered to give them lift in his official car going against the police code. The boy got down en route to the girls place. Later, she was also duly dropped at her home, but not before being allegedly raped by the constable.

The accused cop readily admitted to the sexual intercourse with the girl, but vehemently pleaded that it was a consensual affair. He went to the limit of pleading that she seemed to have enjoyed it tremendously. The court, however, felt that the circumstances of the case spoke otherwise. What weighed against the accused was that there was no need for him to give lift to the couple on any humanitarian grounds, as the alternate conveyance could have been easily available to them even that late in to the night, as the metropolis hardly ever slept. Secondly, the accused knew in advance that the boy would get down first, giving him an opportunity to be with the victim alone. Thirdly, the court was convinced that the girl was not able to raise alarm, as she was in awe of his authority. Finally, there was no earthly reason for the girl to make a false complaint against the accused, as she had no earlier scores to settle with him, In fact, they were the rank strangers.

The London bobby was thus behind the bars undergoing his sentence, well before I left the place. It had taken barely three weeks to carry the case to its logical conclusion. What struck me was the speed with which their system was able to purge itself of its weakness. How one wishes that we could also throw out the rotten eggs in our basket with equal ease and efficiency. What is really stopping us from doing that?

(A reproduction from the writer's article in 'The Hindustan Times' of 3.4.1997.)

49. THE KNIGHTS IN THE SHINING ARMOUR

My first impression of the police as a small child was that they were the knights-at-arms who fought the forces of evil in our society. Thus, when we got information that some criminals were caught, we managed to slip away from our school to the police station not very far away from our place. The only criminals that we could think of those days were the thieves who we thought deserved to be thoroughly thrashed by our heroes, the policemen.

A big log of wood placed in front of the main gate of the 'thana' served as a bench. We vied with one another to occupy a comfortable position on the log and then looked expectantly towards the gate. Mostly, the men in the khaki followed the 'close-door' policy. So, we had to be often content with the sounds alone— the swishes, smacks and shrieks. There were no chinks in the gate for us to view what went inside. When occasionally the gate was left slightly ajar, we could see an unseemly naked body writhing on the ground while being slapped, canned or thrashed with a 'chhittar' (a bigger version of leather sole of a shoe). At that age we thought that all this was fully justified and in fact, it should be done in public. Our image of the police was that of the 'bold and brave' entrusted with the task of ridding the society of the scoundrels.

On one particular day, we got the news that three 'mulzaman' (accused) had been brought to the 'thana' in handcuffs. They had allegedly tried to snatch the 'time-piece' (a small time clock, with facility of alarm) of the 'mehrab' (a revenue official). These functionaries were always at some risk as they had to often work at odd hours to regulate the supply of water from the irrigation channels to various farmers as per their set time schedule. They always carried with them a 'time-piece' for the purpose and in those days, it was considered to be a precious item.

The 'mehrab' in this case was able to raise a timely alarm and the farmers in the nearby fields rushed to his rescue. Thus, all the three culprits were nabbed red-handed without much difficulty. The thieves, it appeared, had already been thoroughly thrashed by the farmers before being brought to the police station. This showed on their bodies physically and was reflected in their state of mind as well. They now looked humble, miserable and completely resigned. After what felt like eternity to us, a A.S.I. (chhota thanedar) emerged from the gate with two heavily built mustachioed constables. We sprang to attentiveness instantaneously, thinking that our sadist urges were soon going to be satisfied. We were, however, up for a surprise.

The A.S.I. had a hard look at the accused. At the end of it, he was probably moved by their plight. He listened patiently to the villagers as well as the accused. The accused admitted their guilt without any fuss and they appeared to be the novices who had already suffered enough. So, there were no fire-works to our great disappointment. The A.S.I. quietly got busy in writing his report.

In between, he suddenly noticed us squirming uneasily on the log. Seeing a look of clear disappointment on our faces, he enquired, "Oye, tuseen soireo kiddan baitheeon?" (Hey, what you little rogues are up to?). We sheepishly replied, "Ji, asaen padhake painde dekhne si" (Sir, we wanted to see the cracker bursts), meaning thereby that we wanted to see the accused thrashed.

The amused A.S.I. clarified that the 'mulzaman' had already got more than their due and moreover, they had admitted to all that they had been accused of. So, the 'padhake' part of it was out. We learnt a very funny thing that day that the police were also human. We withdrew from the place reluctantly cursing the day. However, our playing truant from the class had not proved entirely unproductive. We did come to hear 'padhake' upon our return to the school. Only, this time we were ourselves at the receiving end of the stick at the hands of our school teacher.

(A reproduction from the writer's article in 'The Pioneer' of 11.2.2000.)

50. THE DIFFICULT ART OF LOOKING DAGGERS

If he always got V.I.P. treatment in our home, there were reasons for it. Firstly, he was half a generation ahead of my father. Secondly, he had married my father's sister and men are always entitled to special status in the family they marry in. Thirdly, he was a powerfully built man standing over six feet tall. Finally and most importantly, this Lala Tirath Ram Jhatta, was officer-in-charge of a police-station and looked every bit a 'Thanedar'. He wore an angry young man look most of the time, but when he permitted himself a smile though his thick mustache, he looked to be a real fine picture of man.

He did not like me because of my rebellious nature which would not let me take any nonsense even from men of his stature in the family. He felt rather uncomfortable over the fact that I was the only one around not in adequate awe of his personality. Though he disliked the idea of a paunch, he would, nevertheless, often wonder that how could someone be called a man, if his 'Madhya Pradesh' i.e. the waistline did not measure even 34 inches? At that time, I was a thin and wiry young man, with a waistline matching with that of the film heroines of the day. This was another factor which did not endear me to him. He wanted a proper man to look someone like Satish Shaw or Shivaji Ganeshan of his heyday.

He loved narrating the exploits of his police career, especially his encounters with the dacoits and solving of some difficult investigative riddles. And naturally, he did not like the idea of anybody disturbing him in this dreamy state. Once he was thus turning the pages of his adventurous life, while puffing at his 'hukka' in between. Some small kids were playing close to our courtyard. These young fellows had taken a fancy for a heap of stone-dust piled in a corner where he was sitting. They would climb on to the courtyard wall and jump on the heap in a thud disturbing him seriously in his reverie. Basically nice as he was, he stopped in his tracks temporarily and allowed the kids to have their fun for a while. When the last fellow had his jump, he told them to move on to some other place to play. One obstinate character among them, however, felt that once was not enough and decided to take chance with him.

As he landed noisily on the pile, my Thanedar uncle raised his head over the 'hukka' and threw such a furious look at the little fellow that he nearly froze with fear. He could move only when he was curtly told to get lost. I was deeply impressed and thought that that was how such little rogues should be tackled.

Years went by and I was now a Central Reserve Police officer of the rank of a superintendent of police. I always thought that what a police sub-inspector could do, a police S.P. should be able to do even better. Soon enough I got a chance to try my personality impact.

That day I had a naughty nephew to deal with. He was making a nuisance of himself while I was struggling to finalize an urgent report. I knew that nicety would not cut any ice with him. Still, I called him and told him decently to behave. This was mainly to justify what I intended to do with him next. He expectedly persisted with his boisterousness. I fixed my gaze on his face and tried to assume as stern a look as I could manage. He knew me as a soft and friendly uncle with whom quite a few liberties could be safely taken.

When he found me staring hard at him, he was nonplussed. The young rogue finally looked back at me half-amused, half-confused to enquire innocently why I had suddenly chosen to look like a 'batair' (a bird of the partridge family, known for its idiotic fixed gaze). I felt totally deflated and instantly resolved that I would never again try out such a doltish idea.

(A reproduction from the writer's article in 'The Hindustan Times' of 10.10.1998.)

3

THE DAWN OF FREEDOM

'Bliss was in that dawn to be alive——'

51. THE GREAT SURGE FOR FREEDOM

Patriotism and the urge to overthrow the alien rule were definitely there in the air then. Who or what brought it about — Gandhiji or some incipient impulse rising to the fore — I am not clear about. Sehgal, Dhillon and Shahnawaz, the three Indian National Army officers, had just been released from detention in the Red Fort after being cashiered from the British army. They were the mutineers in the British eyes and would have been routinely put before the firing squads, had their rule not been on its last legs. A massive gathering had been organised at Gol Bagh in Lahore to felicitate them.

The British were still the rulers and they could not bear their cashiered soldiers being raised to the stature of heroes. So, plenty of trouble was anticipated at the venue. This notwithstanding, my father decided to participate. He took even our mother and all of us to the felicitation ceremony. The gathering rent the air with slogans: 'Lal Qile se hue azaad, Sehgal, Dhillon, Shahnawaz'. There were repeated baton charges, but we stood our ground till the very end. Even I, just about nine year old then, did not fail to catch the spirit of the times.

Years later, when I was a B.A. final year student of D.A.V. College, Ambala city (the institution has association with legendary Bhagat Singh and many other martyrs of the Independence struggle), some of us had the privilege of coming in touch with a number of freedom fighters who had suffered terrible tortures at the hands of the British. Another freedom struggle was then going on in the Portuguese-held territory of Goa where our peaceful 'satyagrahi`s' (fighters for justice) were being cruelly suppressed. A number of them got martyred in police firings; some had the soles of their feet scraped; some had their skin cut to inscribe an indelible 'P' on their tonsured heads (to impress the Portuguese authority) and many others were tormented in different other ways.

Five of us in the college felt impelled to join the 'Satyagrah' in Goa in August, 1955. I had to sell my textbooks to raise money for the journey to Pune where a base for the Goa freedom struggle was located. From there, we were dispatched to Belgaum along with many others. The batch intruded into Goa on the night of 30th August. The 'satyagrahi`s' were apprehended and given their share of third degree treatment— some still bear the scars of lashings on their bodies. However, the Portuguese had by now read the writing on the wall and knew that their days in the subcontinent were numbered. So, they released the 'satyagrahi`s' the very next day.

However, what happened back home is more important to me. My mother had been sobbing for me uncontrollably all the time. An elderly Sikh lady from our neighbourhood stopped her sobs instantly by saying, "Nee sher seehnian dey hi paida hunde ne" (Tigers are born to the tigresses only). She instantly decided to live up to the image given to her. As for me, I knew myself to be a most cowardly street-fighter. On return, it was heart-warming for me to learn that I could be a tiger also, where it really mattered.

(A reproduction from the writer's article in 'The Tribune' of 17.1.2011.)

52. THE RISE OF A REPUBLIC

By the time I was born in 1937, some of the battles of our war of Independence had already been won. Independence was now round the corner. It was just a matter of time. The country of the forty crore people having woken up, there was hardly any scope for the British to hang on here. The last two nails in their coffin were driven by their bankruptcy-like plight in the aftermath of the Second World War and the 'Quit India' movement in the subcontinent.

Hope in the air

When the freedom finally dawned on the 15th of August, 1947, quite a few of our freedom fighters, including the ones who had escaped the gallows or the firing squads by a whisker, were still around. I, as a ten year old then, felt something like what Wordsworth had spontaneously said on the breakout of the French Revolution: "Bliss was in that dawn to be alive; to be young was very heaven". The tri-colour flags of the Congress or the triangular saffron flags of the R.S.S. were aflutter on every building that stood in our town. Sadly, all this patriotic exuberance was to be followed by the shame of the Partition.

By 1952, I was a student of the Hans Raj College at Paharganj in New Delhi. Next year on the 26th of January, I got a chance to witness the Republic Day Parade on the Rajpath. The ethos then was entirely different. The crowd at the place was not all that thick as we find these days and the security arrangements were not all that stifling. People could have a much closure look at their leaders and they then had the image of being 'the bravest and the best' among us. Though some smart ones had jumped in to the ring for loaves and fishes of office from out of nowhere and had driven the self-respecting freedom-fighters to the margins, there were hardly any scam tainted figures among them.

The thickest concentration of the crowd formed close to the V.V.I.P. box. After the Parade was formally over, the crowds started melting quickly. Some die-hards like me who were positioned near the Vijay Chowk decided to linger on to have an eyeful at the retreating pageantry. We were not to be disappointed that day. First to come was Dr. Rajendra Prasad, the first President of our Republic, in his horse-driven buggy, folding hands to the people to his right and left in all humility. A few hilarious young men were perched on the edge of the South Block platform with their box-type camera. When they tried to take his picture he happened to sway to the other side. These youngsters shouted to draw his attention towards their camera and he obliged!

He was followed by Pt. Jawahar Lal Nehru, the Prime Minister. There was a surge in the crowd as the smiling Pandit Ji came in view in his open car. The people seemed to be proud to have this handsome man of high calibre as their leader and he got lustily cheered by them. This left no one in doubt as to who the real leader of the nation was at the time.

I really wonder these days when I would next see the similarly lit faces of our people at the sight of our leaders.

(A reproduction from the writer's article in 'The Tribune' of 25.7.2012)

53. THE OLD WORLD CHARM

A newspaper headline about the demise of Satyavati, a centenarian freedom fighter, took my mind back some 55 years. We, a handful of students from D.A.V. College, Ambala city, had then congregated in the rural hinterland of Punjab somewhere around Mansa to participate in the Bhoodaan movement of the late Sant Vinoba Bhave.

The mission in the area was being led by Lala Achint Ram, the husband of this grand old lady who had hid and hosted a number of revolutionaries and national leaders, like Mahatma Gandhi, Nehru, Lajpat Rai, Bhagat Singh and Chandra Shekhar Azad at her residence in Lahore. Achint Ram was then representing the Patiala constituency in our Parliament and Satyavati was present by his side.

We mostly slept under the open skies and dined in a community kitchen run by us. The participants were all spirited and selfless individuals wanting to do something about the inequities in our society in their own humble way. We went from village to village trying to motivate the landed aristocracy to part with at least one sixth of their land holdings in favour of the landless.

It was, indeed, a difficult mission, but quite a few came forward to donate their precious land for the noble cause, because some of the high spirit of our freedom struggle was still alive. Besides, many of the freedom fighters were associated with the movement.

We the students were thus completely caught in the spirit of the camp. In fact, getting charged with a patriotic surge at the place, we actually tried to follow in the footsteps of the freedom fighters in our midst. We were to soon leave for Goa to participate in the 'satyagraha' for its liberation and carry the wounds sustained on our bodies at the hands of the Portuguese police in the spirit of war trophies.

Returning to our Bhoodaan camp, we regularly faced ever-new challenges in our work. We, of course, walked from village to village on foot. However, some transport was always needed to carry our equipment. Once, the mud-track leading to a village that we wanted to cover was completely blocked. Not even a bullock-cart could be driven there.

Finding Lala Ji worried over our getting stranded; we offered to carry the equipment all the way to the village on our person. This sent a visible flutter in his heart. I thus carried a heavy battery on my head. After a few miles, the old man quickened his pace to join me and insisted on sharing the load with me.

By the time I could persuade him to transfer the battery back on my head; he had already covered nearly half a mile. That was the spirit of the times — the times of the grand old couple of the Indian freedom movement.

(A reproduction from the writer's article in 'The Tribune of 30.10.2010)

54. THE PULL OF THE PAST

Everybody is nostalgic about his past. As distant hills look charming, so do the days gone by. With the passage of time, rough edges of life get rounded and a rosy picture of the past gets pasted on our mind, as if we have left a golden era behind.

Earliest memories of my life belong to Jaitu, a marketing town of the erstwhile state of Nabha. We then lived there on the first floor of an old "haveli". When I was around two and a half, my mother undressed me for a bath and then went to the kitchen to fetch warm water. My attention all this while was riveted on a star-studded red cap kept there that I could not wait to wear. I put on the cap and quietly slipped down stairs to the road below. On her return, my mother found me moving among the bullock-carts and camels. Her heart came to mouth and yet, such was then the tradition of "purdah" as held her from coming down to retrieve me.

I witnessed the horrors of partition at the place, with blood and bodies littered in the streets. Then I also saw the flags of freedom proudly fluttering on almost every building in the town on 15th of August, 1947. I am able to recall many more such incidents of my babyhood and boyhood at Jaitu.

This, however, is not the only reason why the place has been showing up in my dreams for the last over 50 years. Jaitu occupies a pedestal of pride in the history of our freedom struggle. It was here that late Pt. Nehru was put in handcuffs during the historic Babbar Akali Movement and taken to Nabha to stand trial before an illiterate magistrate! It is also the place where I, as a curious child, sat before late Giani Zail Singh in a "dharamshala" in one of his election meetings some 60 years back. Giani ji went on to become the First Citizen of our country. Besides, the town was then home to many other freedom fighters like Seth Ram Nath and Mansa Ram who suffered terrible police tortures in the surrounding princely states.

Recently, while returning from my new native place, Bikaner, I got as close to Jaitu as Bhatinda. Though it was then the dead of night and I was booked and bound for Delhi, I could not resist the temptation of visiting the land of my childhood. The next train took me to Jaitu before the dawn broke. Walking in a sort of Arabian Nights trance, I first got to the once imposing circular building in the centre of the town.

Gone were the feared police post, the state bank and other key government offices and gone also was the sentry who struck the gong there 48 times a day. Instead, an ugly shopping complex had cropped up there. I walked in the direction of our "haveli". I had difficulty in even locating the site where it stood. I had similar experience when I went to see my school and other places in my memory. These were all gone or had changed beyond recognition. I looked for acquaintances but could not locate anybody who knew us.

The town seemed to have forgotten us completely. First time I felt that there was no point in looking back in life. I do not think I would see Jaitu in my dreams ever again.

(A reproduction from the writer's article in 'The Tribune' of 3.7.2006.)

55. A CASE OF ADDICTION TO MILK

The early Aryans lived mostly on milk and meat. They, of course, also had high fondness for 'Som Rasa'. This invigorating intoxicant was taken mixed with milk. The cherished drink was lavishly offered to gods and the gatherings on all festive occasions. It has not been possible to identify the plant from which 'Som Rasa' was extracted. This herb, in fact, seems to have gone extinct.

However, thanks to Kurien and his dedicated team, milk continues to flow in our land. In the absence of this timely white revolution triggered by them, we would have by now been drinking the milk prepared out of urea and detergents.

Now, leaving the gone-by millennia behind, I shift to the great sub-continental tragedy, the Partition of 1947. I was then at Jaitu, a politically vibrant town of the erstwhile state of Nabha. There was violence in the air and bodies and blood in the streets.

We lived in a barrack-like house on the first floor of a building that had a number of windows opening on the grain market below. I saw the bullock and camel carts bringing grain, auctions being held and money and grain changing hands peacefully.

Later, through these very windows I was to see an infant girl circling round her mother in deathly panic, crying 'Maa Maa', and both being slaughtered in seconds along with other members of this Muslim family. On top of this, I heard the mob shamefully proclaiming, 'Morcha Fateh' (We have won on this front). The ghastly scene still stays pasted on my mind. Man just seemed caught in a spiral of chain reaction and appeared to have lost his sense of balance. He was just getting tossed about helplessly. When trains started steaming in from the Ferozepur side soaked in Hindu blood, people this side of the divide lost faith in the goodness of human heart and rather thought that violence was perhaps the law of nature and nothing could be done about it. It took considerable time for the sanity to return.

Amid all this, I had an ancestor who reminded me of the Vedic times as he, of all things, was addicted to milk! He was otherwise in the mould of Amir Khusrao, far ahead of his times and perfectly at ease with all religions. It really pained his heart to think what 'man had made of man'.

However, he just could not retire for the day without having a glass of milk. Finding him uncomfortable on this count one evening, my father quietly slipped into the street below littered with bodies and procured a glass of milk for him from a halwai shop. This ancestor of mine took the milk alright realising that it had after all been brought at great risk. However, I do not think that he savoured it as much he usually did.

(A reproduction from the writer's article in 'The Tribune' on 3.2.2010)

4

SOCIAL CONCERNS

India, 'with all thy faults, I love thee still'.

56. 'AAM ADAMI', THE GREAT!

I am an 'aam adami'— negligible, if not totally ignorable and ever open to use and abuse by the high-ups in the society. I am meant to die unhonoured, unwept and unsung. Politicians, no doubt, deem it prudent to keep me on their tongue all the time and pose as if their heart really bleeds over my worries. I may not say it in so my words, but I know them by the marrow of their bones— they are least bothered about my welfare. They just use me as a ladder to get to the top. Once there, they just forget about me.

All this notwithstanding, in a way, I am a highly important entity also. My power lies in my numbers. Numbers, when they collect and coalesce together, bring to life a magic of their own. After all, nobody can out-people the people in this world. The richest man on earth cannot have the money and means that I collectively have. Besides, I hide a revolution within on the quiet. When I sleep, I am weak. When I rise, the high and mighty run for cover— Charles's get beheaded, Louis's get guillotined, Shaw's get kicked out of their countries and Prime Ministers are made to eat a humble pie.

I agree that I am a bit of an idiot myself. I get easily taken in when the opposition parties perennially raise the bogey of inflation, without relating the rising prices to the extra money pouring in my pocket because of the rapid expansion of the currency in circulation. Similarly, I readily fall for the 'Reserve and Rule' policy of the political outfits without understanding its implications for national growth. They are thus able to deceive me by coining ever new slogans election after election.

However, I may appear to care very little about what goes on around me, yet I do not fail to take notice of what concerns my life, livelihood and self-respect. All this just keeps collecting inside me and simmering there silently. I do not mind paying taxes so long the money comes back to me as schools, hospitals, roads, delivery of security and justice and so on. I certainly feel indignant when the billions are wasted on leaky plans like the Twenty-point programme, loan-waivers, rural employment, food security schemes and distribution of free electricity and other goodies etc., designed primarily to garner my vote. I know for sure that a large chunk of this money is going to disappear in greedy pockets and foreign banks.

Anyway, when I get unbearably distressed over injustice, crime, corruption and enslavement of my spirit, there rise out of me the likes of Oliver Cromwell, George Washington, Mahatma Gandhi, Jai Prakash Narain and Anna Hazare etc. to dust the societies clean of sin and inappropriateness. This phenomenon finds an echo in the Bhagawat Geeta when Lord Krishna declares: "whenever righteousness gets trampled and inappropriateness comes to the fore, I incarnate myself in the world from age to age to bring succour to the pious, to destroy sinful propensities and to restore faith of the people in righteousness". The politicians and others ever ready to exploit me should understand that Krishna here is speaking for me or I am is the Krishna Himself speaking here.

I, as an 'aam adami', am not important just for my vote in a democratic set up, even the dictators fear me and rule with me and God on their lips all the time, though they otherwise care little for the either.

(A reproduction from the writer's article in 'The Tribune' of 2.1.2013)

57. CONDITIONS APPLY

Corruption really runs deep in our system and people are absolutely fed up with this state of affairs. It, however, is not limited to politicians and bureaucrats alone. It permeates our entire society.

A few years back, I purchased an air-conditioner from a company that promised that I would be provided three-day free stay for two in hotels at different destinations within or outside the country according to my choice. After the purchase, the shopkeeper assured me that I would soon receive vouchers from the company in performance of their promise.

As they appeared to have conveniently forgotten about their commitment, I reminded them about it and they did send me the vouchers loaded with their conditions. I was to pay a substantial amount towards service charges, give them a long notice with three choices in terms of destinations and the time period and certain premium periods were out-of-bounds for me. I complied with all these.

There was no response from the representatives of the company till the last moment. It was abundantly clear to me that besides the escalated price of the AC with the lure attached to it, it had also misappropriated some more money in the name of service charge for the promised tour. The notice that I gave them for their fraudulent ways was taken by them in their stride.

I had to thus file a case against them in the District Consumer Forum which has its own requirements. I was first told to have my petition retyped leaving sufficient space on the top for the forum to do some scribbling and also attach a postal order for Rs 100 with it. I complied with this all. The forum then demanded that I should produce the copy of the advertisement of the company offering free stay for tours. This had already been trashed by me. But, as an advocate, I was able to convince the forum that the promise to provide free stay at various destinations was, indeed, made by the company.

They kindly agreed to issue a notice to them. However, their office insisted that they were out of funds and I should issue the notice on their behalf myself. They, however, agreed to put the stamps of the forum on the envelopes.

This finally made the company to offer me free stay for the promised tour and also five thousand rupees towards expenses. I, thus, got even with them so far as my own case was concerned. But, all this left me thinking that it was a rather easy getaway for the fraudulent company. They should have been proceeded against criminally, as they must have made substantial money by duping others. It was thus abundantly obvious to me that corruption was not limited to the governments — the whole of the country was knee deep in it. This is how Anna has emerged as the darling of the nation today.

(A reproduction from the writer's article in The Tribune' of 2.9.2011)

58. THE STORIES WITHOUT AN END

We, particularly our housewives, are being entertained to scores of feisty serials by a host of TV channels. Often they run to hundreds of episodes and are concluded only when the viewers start feeling totally exasperated with their scripts going increasingly wayward with every passing day. It is eventually the reducing volume of their viewership that decides their ultimate story. The producers, at this stage, quickly bring their serials to an abrupt end on the principle: *"Woh afsana jise anjam tak lana na ho mumkin, use ek khoobsurat morh de kar chhodna achha"* (If it is not possible to take a story to its logical end, it is better to abandon it midway by giving it an interesting twist).

If the scripts of these serials are finally consolidated into a novel, these would beat any of our great epics in terms of their size. However, the only problem is that they would not make any sense, simply because no cross-thread of cohesion runs through these from the beginning to the end. Their episodes are in the nature of a few disjointed clusters of stories. One has to rip one's attention apart from the previous bunch to latch on to the next one.

Some 30 years back, I read an article suggesting that Rani Padmini of Chittor, who sits on our psyche as a sort of a national heroine, was a fictional character. This gave me a jolt and I decided to investigate her historicity. After a study lasting decades and countless trips to all sorts of weird places, I was able to piece together sufficient evidence to conclude that she was, in fact, a historical reality.

Before my book on the subject appeared on the shelves, I was approached by a TV production house to write a serial on Rani Padmini for them. I accordingly produced a five-episode script for their consideration. I was urged to stretch the serial to at least 13 episodes. Inexperienced as I then was, I put my foot down on the ground that the story in that case would become insipidly slow-moving. I did not realise that, in any case, half the time in the episodes would go to the advertising slots. My unnecessary stubbornness finally killed the project.

With the hindsight, I now feel that I should not have fussed about the crispness of the story. What after all could be wrong if I had showed a bunch of "sahelis" (female friends) of the superlative lady stripping her for the bath in the water body surrounding her palace. Possibilities in the area were, in fact, endless. Sadly, I failed to seize upon these.

(A reproduction from the writer's article in 'The Tribune' of 13.6.2012.)

59. ABOUT A FADED PASSION

Nargis Dutt

I do not recall having seen a movie in a theatre since 1977 and so far as multiplexes are concerned, I do not even have any idea what they look like from inside. Of course, this was not the case with me in my childhood. I was then a different being.

Even before entering my teens I had got obsessed with films. In the late forties of the last century, actress Suraiya had emerged as the most sensational heroine of the silver screen. What added to her appeal was her prodigious singing talent — she was, for a while, rated ahead of Lata. I, however, found actress Nargis in a more perfect classical mould and got attracted to her. By the age of 11, I had already acquired the capacity to write readable English. One can easily understand my euphoria when my letter to Nargis was thus able to elicit a reply from her under her own signatures.

She had, of course, written that she was happy to note that I wanted to become a film actor. She was, however, quick to add that it was, by no means, an easy life. I shot back in my next letter that I was determined to come good in this line however hard the life might be. This letter and a few more that followed from me got no reply. Her only letter that I received had to be kept hidden from my father. It is doubtful if he knew much about Nargis, but putting two and two together he would have come to know what I was up to. So the highly classified document remained secretly tucked in the sleeve of my 'pyjama' for many months, till it got dropped somewhere to my great dismay.

In the meantime, I got two of my friends interested in going to Bombay for a career in films. They were elder to me by good many years, yet I was their undisputed ring-leader. All three of us made to Mumbai, but only I could manage to meet Nargis. Not to speak of Sanjay who was yet to be born, even Sunil Dutt was not in the reckoning then.

Nargis lived in a ground floor apartment on the Marine Drive in a bungalow by the name of 'Chateau Marine'. I went to her place and was fascinated to see a nameplate on her door — Miss Fatima Rashid Nargis. Next, I used the abundant histrionic talents of a child when her servant tried to remove me from the place. So he had to take me inside. Once in, a kindly young girl (I was to see her later on the screen as Zubaida) led me by the hand straight to the bedroom of Nargis. We were, of course, asked post haste to wait in the drawing-room. Nargis appeared there after a few minutes. She looked much prettier than her image on the screen. She was able to talk me out of my obsession with the film career in minutes and send me back to pursue my course to the armed forces, where I really belonged.

(A reproduction from the writer's article in 'The Tribune' of 28.5.2011)

60. THE MURDER OF A MORNING

We were then trying to come to terms with our post-retirement life. I could have hung on to my orderlies for some more time. But we took a conscious decision to break with our service life and settle down to a self-reliant future.

One implication of that for me was to get up early in the morning and go to the Mother Dairy booth about a kilometre from our place. Despite my long service in the armed forces, I had somehow not got in the habit of rising early. I did so only when it was absolutely necessary. Now again, it was time when I had to be per force up on my feet at dawn.

However, those few of us who do get up early know that it was not for nothing that it was said, "Bliss was in that dawn to be alive". There is an indescribable freshness in the morning air that puts you in that mysterious "feel good" mood. You somehow come to believe that "God is in heaven and all is well with the world". You find the dust of the gone-by day calmly settled and the new day has yet to raise its quota of dust and noise.

Even 20 years back, there were millions of motorised vehicles on the Delhi roads. The advent of the Metro has, indeed, shaved of some of the traffic from the roads, but a sustained influx of people in the Capital over the years and the pathetic state of public transport have ensured that the roads here remain as jam-packed as these were then.

In fact, some regional politicians who do not see any chance of coming good at the national level have been making life difficult for the outsiders in their vote catchment areas. The national Capital is the only place where every Indian has an inalienable right to stay and work. Hence this heartland of the nation acts as a magnet to draw a constant stream of people from all corners of the country.

With a stainless steel "dolu"' (a cylindrical bucket) in hand and the above thoughts in head, I was quietly moving towards the booth with the atmospheric ozone and serenity keeping me company and giving me hope that all would be well in the end. Suddenly an old and ill-kept Matador appeared from behind bellowing a thick cloud of smoke. The vehicle disappeared in a matter of seconds, but the bitter smoke that it emitted hung on the entire length of the road. All that was good about the morning was gone.

The feeling of peace and tranquility was simply shattered. Forgetting completely about the morning freshness, I now found myself fighting off the smoke. A single polluting vehicle had, thus, killed my morning and another ugly day stood staring at me.

(A reproduction from the writer's article in 'The Tribune' of 3.3.2008.)

61. PANIC AT PALWAL

British were still in command of our country, but their rule was on its last legs. I was then just around nine and my family was residing at Jaitu, a commercial town of the princely state of Nabha. Our railway station was a sort of socialising spot. We went there almost every day to spend our evenings in gossip, munching a "papad" or chewing a "pan", if our pockets permitted.

The trains then used to have four classes for the passengers—the Third, for the Tom, Dick and Harry's like us, the Inter, for the slightly better placed, prepared to pay one and a half times of the normal fare, the Second, mostly for the government servants travelling at government cost and the First, almost exclusively for the British. The passenger trains stopped at the railway station mostly for a minute or so and the coaches used to be often overcrowded.

Once a passenger train arrived at the station and the passengers rushed to board it. A bunch of rustic women from a nearby village got into an inter-class compartment in their hurry. One of them then noticed the cushioned seats and shouted breathlessly "Nee dudhe karaey wali hai" (O, you, it is a compartment carrying one and a half times fare). Meanwhile, the train started coming to motion. The women in their panic almost jumped from the moving train. This reflected the awe in which the government and the law were then held.

Nearly 50 years later, when I was travelling in a reserved coach of a mail train bound for Delhi, one of the passengers made the mistake of opening the door at one of the nearby stations in the early hours of the morning. A swarm of commuters floated into the bogie demanding the sleeping passengers to make room for them. The overawed passengers helplessly complied. The groups of unruly commuters then made themselves comfortable here and there. They started playing cards and engaged themselves in noisy discussions, interspersed with filthy words, least bothered about the presence of lady passengers around them.

When I tried to get up to confront them my wife weighed me down by clinging to my side. She wisely said that when the Railway Minister and the Prime Minister had failed to deal with this so common a scenario, what chance I stood of succeeding here.

The other day I saw the telecast of the mayhem in a reserved railway coach of Bhopal Express. Some goons had got into it at Palwal and misbehaved with the lady passengers. On being resisted, they got violent and are said to have tried to roast the passengers alive by setting fire to the coach. The worried faces of the innocent women who had jumped from the moving train at Jaitu, just because they had boarded a wrong bogie by mistake, flashed before my eyes.

Surely, the fear of the law is largely gone and the respect for the law is yet to take its place. There are some elements among us who feel that they can merrily go for rioting and rapes and some goon whom they have placed in a position of power through their vote, would shield them. Surely, the country has been driven to a state where we desperately need to barter some of our democracy for discipline.

(A reproduction from the writer's article in 'The Tribune' of 18.3.2008.)

62. AN INAUGURATION

We, indeed, are a God-fearing and thrifty people with high IQ. We can also take pride in the fact that we have been able to solve many of our intractable problems related to food grain production, milk, telecommunications, etc, courtesy the brilliant sons of this soil like Swaminathan, Kurien and Sam Pitroda. But among many things, both good and bad, we are also apparently a nation of bootlickers. Far too many inaugurations and too little action on the ground provide a testimony to this trait. Here is the story of one such inauguration in the capital of the country.

A VIP was coming to the area to inaugurate, of all things, a garbage bin! The invitation to him was justified on the ground that a bin of an entirely new pattern was being introduced. A few municipal officials were lined up there with marigold garlands in their hands. Some onlookers also stood at the scene half-confused and half amused.

There was a shamiana on the spot where items like gulab jamuns, chhaina murgi (cubes of cheese with sugar coating) and cashew nuts were already laid while jalebis, samosas and pakoras were waiting for the news about the VIP as these were intended to be served hot. The people in the gathering who hoped to join the feast were sticking to the site steadfastly, whereas the other collected merely out of curiosity were just coming and going.

The VIP was already late by a couple of hours. At long last, when his cavalcade was spotted, the officials swung into action. A newspaper was shredded and the pieces scattered on the ground. After being felicitated with garlands and artificial smiles, he was handed over a broom to clean the area of the pieces of paper and then to deposit these ceremonially in the bin. The VIP rather made a good job of all this.

An amused spectator snidely remarked that that was what the man should have been normally doing. The pungency of the remark was not lost on the officials who heard him. They gave him a caustic look, but soon got busy in the more important task of carrying a jug of water, a washbasin and a towel to the VIP to enable him to wash and wipe his hands.

Something was now needed to be said about the municipal officials who had so painstakingly arranged the show. This comment was also not very late in coming. Someone from among the spectators suggested that the VIP should sweep these fellows also into the bin as garbage. Their jaw momentarily fell over this public reaction. But they soon realised that their career needed the blessings of the VIP, and the wretched public really did not matter. So, they happily left for the dining table behind the VIP.

(A reproduction from the writer's article in 'The Tribune' of 14.12.2004.)

63. A VALUED CLIENT

My elder son, a businessman engaged in air-ticketing, is always in shortage of the working capital. Money is, thus, welcome to him from whatever source and at whatever cost it comes. Occasionally, he has to borrow money from the market at as high a rate as 48 per cent P.A. This being his situation and state of mind, he is a sought after person with the banks on the look-out for profitable outlets for their surplus funds.

My son often gets referred to as a "valued client" in their letters. They do not just do it out of formality. They, indeed, know what they are writing. Where else would you find a ready borrower who pays you interest perennially at the rate of 35 per cent P.A., often along with decent penalties for not paying even the mandatory 5 per cent of the credit card purchases and other instalments in time?

Once he, out of curiosity or perhaps need also, tried to see if he could get away by not paying the dues of a bank. After a couple of months of default, a telephone call came from the headquarters of the bank at Bangalore, first trying to know if I was Shekhar, my son. I informed that I was his daddy. The man claimed that he was speaking from the Karnataka High Court where a criminal case had been filed against my son for bouncing of a cheque.

When I told him that I happened to be an advocate of the Supreme Court and enquired how a case of cheque bouncing had directly landed in the High Court, he at once came to the point and instead requested if I could advise my son suitably. This was done and the issue settled. It also became adequately evident to my son that, at his level of smartness, it was not possible to get a bank off his back. The point went home.

In my own case, no bank offers to remit or even reduce the annual charges on my credit card, as I would neither make sizeable purchases from their sponsored shops nor afford them an opportunity to earn 35 per cent P.A. and penalties in addition. To their great dislike, I make it a point to make all payments in time. Even if they occasionally refer to me also as their "valued client", they really do not mean it.

With the post-office deposit schemes lately turning unattractive, the money has again started streaming into the banks. However, deposits sans their profitable deployment do not make sense. Herein lies the importance of the likes of my son. His dismal record in the matter of repayments notwithstanding, the banks are keen to do business with him and are always eager to enhance his limits and offer him incentives. After all, he does pay in the end through his nose.

(A reproduction from the writer's article in 'The Tribune' of 14.12.2004.)

64. BREAST-BEATING FOR THE POOR

I am no votary of socialism, particularly of our kind. In fact, I am of the view that it is our obsession with this socialism that held us back nearly for four decades. In our skewed thinking socialism meant that the people should be allowed to set up slums wherever they liked, permitted to steal electricity from the overhead wires in full government view and they should have the privilege of easing themselves on the adjoining footpaths and so on.

Yet, despite all the breast-beating that our politics has done for their benefit, it is more or less clear that nobody's heart bleeds for the poor. Delhi has been developing ever new colonies for its burgeoning population. One of its newest townships is the Dwarka sub-city meant for around a million people. In the good old days, some ruler established a town of twenty-five thousand and left his name by it. Setting up a city of one million certainly needs some doing. Those who have done it deserve appreciation and applause.

Sadly, however, the cause of the poor was totally ignored while bringing this conglomerate into being. The powers-that-be behaved as if these poor were non-citizens, not entitled to any civic rights. None realised that they were also socially useful beings. First, quite a few thousand of them had to be around as a labour force to raise nearly two lakh dwelling units. Secondly, our middle class has not reached a stage where vacuum cleaners can take over "jharu-pocha" and dish-washers, the "bartan Manjana" chores. So, maids invariably have to be a part of our social milieu for another decade or so. Thirdly, somebody has to ply rickshaws, set up fruit/vegetable stalls and provide a plethora of other so-called menial services. Why should such socially relevant people not be catered for?

Dwarka looks to be one of the most livable places in the capital now. However, when I shifted here some six years back it had the appearance of a haunted locale as soon as the night fell. There was no habitation within a radius of half a kilometre of my housing society, where we lived alone with just construction labourers for company. I saw them cluttered into small make-shift hutments, devoid of any ventilation. Their men and women had to bath together at a common water tap. Their babies had to lie or move about unattended for hours. Their small children passed time rolling junk wheels with a stick.

Maid servants came from their far off 'jhuggi`'s paying through nose. Vegetable sellers and tea-vendors etc got routinely chased away by the police every other day. Being a direct witness to their plight, I often wondered if our politicians' concern for them was not just about election-deep. In this ethos, one would always remain apprehensive about bulk of the massive money earmarked for our well-intentioned Rural Employment Scheme instead ending up in greedy pockets.

(A reproduction from the writer's article in 'The Tribune' of 12.10.2005.)

65. THE AGE OF THE SHOWMAN

There are a few persons in our midst who display ability, do hard work, are considered key people for a long while, but eventually end up without recognition of any sort. They always remain in an illusion that their work would speak for them. Unfortunately, silences rarely speak. Merit and sincerity alone do not add up to much — not any longer at least. Ours is the age of the showman as never before.

Late Raj Kapur, the choicest gene of the Kapur clan and the brightest light of the tinsel world, was often referred to as the "showman". Far from being so, he was a man lost in his work. He was certainly not the best actor of his time, but look at his overall contribution — all the movies with soulful themes and lilting music that he has left behind. The coveted 'Dada Sahib Phalke Award' did come his way, but just when he was dying and unable to move from his seat— our gracious President had to go to him to bestow the honour. Had he really been a showman many minister ships and other such rewards would have been his for the asking.

Again, think of the obscure man who created the hilarious "Hey Jamalo" that triggered what has come to be known as 'indipop'. The man has vanished in the shadows because he was not able to market himself. But for others, this has meant notes and notice all the way.

At more earthly levels, my father was an excellent teacher. He exactly knew how to make minds receptive for learning. I know it firsthand because I happened to be his student for good many years. I remember that he, while once taking our geography class referred to the lines of longitude and latitude as imaginary lines. Then, to check back, he told us that one of the longitude lines passed close to our neighbouring village. He offered to take us there for picnic and also, of course, to let us have look at it. All of us sprang to attention with curiosity. After rather an embarrassingly long bout of sheepishness, we finally realised that imaginary lines could not exist on the ground and these were meant for maps only. I do not think any of us has forgotten about it since then.

However, showmanship was just not there in the system of my father. So, he never got any kind of recognition for his superlative teaching ability and had to be content with the job satisfaction that he felt within.

Today, our females are freely coming forward to display every part of their anatomy, except for the last few square inches (in fact, the internet has put even this forbidden area universally in-bound). The pop singers are busy producing albums based on just anything that they think would catch the tired popular imagination— the flickering lights, the glimpses and gyrations of female flesh, the hitherto unknown mysteries of vocal chords, colours, outlandish hair-styles, funny dresses and in fact, anything that the fun-loving folks would pay for. What sort of music is it is that needs such a gigantic extraneous support?

Now, how long this age of the showman is going to last—perhaps, forever. The tastes and techniques may change, but basic parameters will remain the same. More of a man after all lives in his mind. So, marketing shall always be important. Showmanship will keep casting its long shadow over sincerity and merit in all ages. I really wonder if raw truth ever prevailed. In fact, showmanship seems to have been the truth all through, though there has to be, indeed, some substance in the folds of showmanship also.

(A reproduction from the writer's article in 'The Tribune' of 17.6.2004.)

66. THE THREE ON TWO WHEELS

In Delhi, the capital of perhaps the most liberal democracy of the world, you often see three uncouth-looking youth riding a two-wheeler at great speed, honking all the while, flailing their arms in ecstasy, letting all sorts of sounds to amuse the persons passing by and believing innocently that the traffic regulations do not apply to them. I tell you, they are a great sight— at least, this is what they think of themselves. They seem to believe that the road all but belongs to them. After all, the person from whom they have borrowed the bike must have paid his road taxes.

For some reason, they are always in a tearing hurry. Perhaps the bike is available to them only for a while and their idea is to enjoy their short ride to the hilt. They weave their way deftly through the traffic, riskily and noisily startling one and all. But this does not ruffle many feathers because we are such a patient lot that we can take all sorts of nuisance and noise in our stride. Even when much of traffic is not there, they drive in such a curly manner as would put a 'nagin' (female snake) to shame.

Once I saw one of these threesomes riding a scooter in Dwarka sub-city of Delhi. They were driving on the wrong side, and, as usual, at quite some speed. To top it all, the one who was driving had a mobile tucked between his right shoulder and head and he was talking on it all the while. Often he felt the need of taking away his right hand from the handle to adjust the ever-slipping mobile.

As luck would have it, a truck appeared in front of them rather suddenly. The truck was on its right side and more importantly, it was being driven by one who after all was a truck driver. He drove it close to the scooter in a manner that brought its riders to the mother earth instantly. Their mobile was cast quite a distance away. The bike grazed against the divider hissing angrily and finally skidded on the ground. Its riders fell front-rolling over each other in the manner of judo fighters. The truck driver got down, held them by the shoulder one by one and brought them to their feet.

They now looked lost and bewildered. Someone recovered their mobile and put it in the listless hands of one of them. It took some time for their vacant looks to get into a properly seeing mode. Fortunately, there were no fractures. But they had bruises all over. However, it was not the bruises that bothered them. It was the visible damage to the borrowed bike that was worrying them no end.

(A reproduction from the writer's article in 'The Tribune' of 4.8.2010.)

67. A TALE OF THREE CITIES

Somebody said: "England, with all thy faults I love thee still". We, the Indians, feel no differently, though our faults are far too many for comfort. It is not without a certain amount of shame over our poor road etiquettes that I recount below the three road accidents, to which I was a witness, in the cities of London, Paris and our own, New Delhi. These say all.

The first of these occurred while I was on my return journey to London after a visit to France. Our bus driven by one Nick collided with a car in Paris. Fortunately, no one was injured. Going by the type of police response that we have in our own country in case of road accidents, I had a sinking feeling. I thought we would be stuck at the spot for hours and then in the end our vehicle might be impounded, leaving us to our own devices to go back. After all, vehicles from two different countries were involved in the accident.

But, this is what actually happened. Nobody, except the drivers, got down from the vehicles. In a matter of minutes, a French Police car appeared on the scene out of nowhere. They examined the scene of accident and asked both the vehicles to pull to the extreme right of the road (France, like the bulk of the world, is a right hand drive country). Nick returned to the bus and requested a French-knowing lady to come down and help him in explaining his case to the police. She readily obliged. In around 20 minutes of the accident, we were on way to London again.

During my recent visit to Britain, two cars driven by ladies banged into each other close to our residence on Ashford Road. They came out and wished each other. They then rang up the police and in the meanwhile exchanged information about their insurance policies. They spent a few minutes before the arrival of the police in friendly conversation. With the police formalities over, they went their ways shaking hands warmly. Thus, London and Paris, more or less, stood at the same high pedestal in the matter of civil behaviour, their serious politico-lingual rivalries notwithstanding.

The third accident that I witnessed occurred in Delhi. There were again no injuries and not much damage to the cars involved. Still, two fellows bolted out of the vehicles fuming and flew to the throat of each other, each presuming that the fault lay entirely with the other. Nearly 50 spectators collected in a circle round them to see the fun. It required quite some sane effort to separate the two agitated boors. Finally they withdrew to their cars, still gnashing and growling at each other. Obviously, they hardly had any faith in the police or law in the matter of dispute resolution and were keen to settle the matters on the spot.

Our stable family life and many other social values are the envy of the West. Why are we then losing out on the civilisational scale on such silly counts?

(A reproduction from the writer's article in 'The Tribune' of 27.10.2008.)

68. THE BIGGER EVIL

'Kuchh bhi na kaho'— This wonderful cartoon says it all.

Our country ranks quite high in the matter of corruption. We can, nonetheless, take comfort from the fact that we are in good company. Some prominent countries like Russia, China and Pakistan are, more or less, at the same level.

In fact, Lord Clive & Warren Hastings who laid such a strong foundation of the British Empire in India were the known corrupts and were duly put to shame for this back home. Yet, they kept the interest of the empire above theirs and did nothing that would damage the clout of their country.

Our corruption, however, has a different dimension. It is intermixed with inefficiency and arrogance. Government officials here do not think that they are the paid servants of the people. They consider themselves as part of the ruling establishment and the people as their subjects.

The other day the members of a group housing society in the country's capital were waiting for the allocation of their flats through the draw of lots. As per the prevailing practice, the draw had to be managed by some officials from the office of the Registrar of Co-operative Societies and the local development authority. There was no trace of these worthies at the appointed time. The members of the society that included Air Marshal Brar, the then Vice Chief of the Indian Air Force, were getting restive. The embarrassed prime-mover of the society was pacing up and down muttering that they would definitely come as all their demands had been met.

After keeping everybody waiting for over two hours a bunch of half a dozen blokes led by an official of hardly Under Secretary's rank appeared on the scene. In the manner of a minister, the senior officer apologized to the gathering for delay, but wanted them to appreciate how busy (read important) they were. The half amused and half confused members felt like shoe-beating them out of the complex, but remained quiet keeping their helpless situation in view. So, the bribes in our country are not collected as crumbs but are extracted as tributes. Like the hated levy of "Zazia" in some periods of the Muslim rule these are required to be paid in all humility.

These days some ten thousand members of the housing societies in Delhi are in intense agony. Their flats have been ready for years but they are not being allowed to occupy these, statedly for judicial reasons. Though there is no court stay in the case the very pendency of even a remotely connected matter there provides good enough an excuse for those unwilling to work.

In this context, an exasperated old man, waiting long to move to his fully paid for home, recently remarked that the previous Registrar (now in jail for allegations of corruption) was preferable to the present one. The fellow might have indulged in corruption, but at least the things were moving during his time. The old man might have been carried away by his desperation, but he had perhaps said it. Inefficiency, indeed, is a bigger evil than even corruption.

(A reproduction from the writer's article in "The Tribune' of 25.12.2006.)

69. THE STATE OF THE NATION

Over a period of time, numerous side-stories have got woven around some episodes of our epics. These seemingly superficial stories are sometimes loaded with considerable meaning and depth. I narrate below a typical tale that hangs by an incident of 'Ramayana'. Its value lies in its satirical import and comment on the contemporary situation.

Eager to see that his illustrious father, Dasratha, was able to keep his word in the finest traditions of the 'Raghu' dynasty, his devoted son , Rama, happily accepts the sentence of spending fourteen years in the solitude of 'vanas' (forests). Incidentally, the term of fourteen years became an important entity in our penal system. For a long while, India was under the Islamic criminal laws that provided for amputation of one or two limbs for certain crimes. The British converted the punishment of amputation of two limbs (left hand and right leg) in to rigorous imprisonment for fourteen years. As per our Supreme Court ruling, a person sentenced to life imprisonment must spend at least fourteen years in prison. The next punishment is fourteen years in jail which may, of course, get reduced substantially as a result of periodic remissions.

Rama was, however, an innocent victim, much loved by the citizenry of Ajodhya. His subjects followed him to the banks of 'Saryu' river, much to his embarrassment. Finally, acting tough, he issued what we now call a 'farman', 'fatwa' or 'hukam nama' that all men and women would go back to Ajodhya to resume their routine life. After this, he with his wife and brother, who had decided to cast their lot with him, quietly crossed 'Saryu' and vanished in the 'vanas'. Next morning, all the men and women assembled on the bank of 'Saryu' left for Ajodhya, as ordained. However, those who were neither men nor women, decided to stay put in the absence of any directions for them.

Rama, thus, found a colony of Hizras (eunuchs) at the place when he returned after fourteen years. Greatly moved by their love and devotion, he blessed them with a boon that they would also get an opportunity to rule the land one day. Hizras were to later give an excellent account of themselves as guardsmen for the harems and also prove their worth in the area of public entertainment. One of them, Malik Kafur, rose to the stature of the Naib Sultan of the country and even ruled as a regent for a few months. Thus, Rama's commitment to them was met as early as the fourteenth century.

However, one feels that the proper Hizra rule is, in fact, on now (No offence meant to the Hizras). How else can one explain people stealing electricity from the overhead wires in full government view, setting up slums wherever they feel like and easing themselves on the adjoining footpaths, a country one seventh of our size threatening us over Kashmir for years and the land of Ellora, Ajanta, Taj and Qutab with a recorded history of five millennia attracting far less tourists than those who alight in the tiny city state of Singapore and, in general, the crows feeding on pearls while the swans starve?

(A reproduction from the writer's article in 'The Hindustan Times' of 1.11.1999.)

70. A LEAF FROM AN OPEN BOOK

During the general elections of 1977, the companies and outposts of my 51st Battalion, C.R.P. Force were scattered all over Saurashtra. The region has quite a few heritage sites to offer to a tourist and in fact, also to a student of history. This provided me an opportunity to have a look at some of these places of emotional, spiritual and historic significance. Located on the sea shore to the west and a close by island are the temples and palaces believed to be associated with Lord Krishna. It is one of the four 'dhams' (abodes of God) that have been the silent symbols of the spiritual unity of Hindus and of the territorial integrity of this country for many millennia. Down south stands the historic Somnath temple that has risen phoenix-like in all its glory after being repeatedly vandalized around a millennium back by the hordes of Mahmud Ghaznavi and having remained in a near derelict state since then till the dawn of our Independence.

Its Gir forest is home to the Asiatic lion. The Gir lions appear to have been nearly domesticated. Often these are called close to the road side with the bait of a calf for the tourists to have a look at them from as close a distance as twenty yards. The forest guards, with their guns casually slung on their shoulders, stand close to the calf with a small stick or rather a twig in their hands. As the lions show an inclination to pounce on the calf, the guards just place the stick on its back to indicate to the hopeful lions, "Not today, dears". Curiously, the lions submissively stop in their track. Then, there is Jam Nagar known once for its solarium and now pulsating with industrial activity. Following the shore line towards the south, one gets to the ancient sea port of Porbander. Despite all the stink from the catches of fish here and there, the place now wears a sort of halo around it, because it happens to be the birth place of Mahatma Gandhi.

Of all these fascinating destinations, what lingers in my mind is the visit to the Mahatma's mansion (haveli) at Porbander. The place preserves many of the memories associated with this saintly politician, the likes of whom put up an appearance once in ages. The spots where he was delivered, studied and played have been carefully indicated. Not very far, at the back of this mansion, stands the parental home of Kasturba.

By the side of the Gandhiji's home a unique shrine has come up. Its uniqueness does not lie in its composite culture alone. Of course, it has the combined architectural touch of a Hindu temple, a Muslim mosque, a Sikh Gurudwara and a Christian Church. But what really touches a person's heart is its sanctum sanctorum, where a largish book is kept. The place itself is open and windy that makes the leaves of the book flutter frequently. When you realize why exactly the book is placed at the holy spot, the ambience of this openness strikes you with all the more intensity. The book signifies the transparent life of the Mahatma! You could turn any page of his life and read it to know what the man was like. He was, of course, also human and no human can be above sin. However, if the Mahatma rarely happened to commit a sin, he would never hide it and let it rot inside. He always had an urge to purge his soul of it as quickly as possible.

When I read the details about the Clinton-Lewinsky intrigue, the memories of the place came rushing back to me. So, the high a mighty also have bones and blood inside and often lot to hide. Leave alone the ordinary mortals, even the bravest and the best find it hard to get to that nothing-to hide state. It makes me wonder if the world would not be a lot better place to live, if all statesmen borrowed at least a page from the life of this humble Mahatma. There would not then be so much sin and strife around us.

(A reproduction from the writer's article in 'The Hindustan Times' of 10.11.1998.)

71. THE CHEER LEADERS!

Pope Gregory the Great (AD 540-604) once saw some young English slaves sold in to slavery in a Roman market. As per the prevailing practice, they were exhibited for sale naked. Gregory who was then only a Benedictine monk was so impressed with their beauty and grace that he spontaneously remarked:-

"Non Angli, sed Angeli sunt" (They are not English, but angels)

He instantly thought of going to England to convert the country to Christianity. Somehow he could not make it. The task was left to his successors.

Let us move our mind now to a bunch of scantily clad shapely females, perched on a dais in one corner of a cricket field, doing dutifully what they are paid to do— dancing wildly, as if in a truly ecstatic stance over the hitting of boundaries, flailing limbs, smiling mechanically all the while, blowing kisses all around, receiving lustful glances and lewd remarks from the spectators. The scene of the Roman slave market of the millennia gone by is right in front of you. Bodies may not be at sale here, but beauty certainly is. Are they there to give you your money's worth or they just reflect artificiality and unnaturalness?

While the game is on, the cameras often cut to some naturally expressive faces of the sleeping babies, amused young women, old folks enjoying the game, relaxed looking V.I.P.'s and lustily cheering youth. Some come here with funnily painted faces, masks and placards to invite the attention of the cameras on themselves. There is always some newness and freshness in the expressions of joy, astonishment and disappointment on these faces in the crowd. Some could even be noticed praying for their side visibly. All this is amusing and enjoyable.

On the other hand, the artless gestures of the cheer leaders, repeated over and over again, are just boring. It is only their glamour quotient—beautiful faces, well-endowed busts and shapely thighs that interest the spectators. The feel-good factor about them may be more effectively at work in the post match parties, where the players and the selected guests have a chance for a closer interaction with them.

Why do these well-endowed ladies fall on one another to get picked up as cheer leaders? It could not be for the money alone. Perhaps these young women are equally keen on visibility in the audio-visual media. It is though doubtful if this exposure in any way promotes their careers in the field of modeling, television and films etc. They really do nothing here in terms of dialogue delivery, facial expressiveness and other gestures to give a glimpse of their acting talents.

True, as Wordsworth says, "a thing of beauty is joy forever". These pretty damsels can create a great feel-good ethos among the spectators and the T.V. viewers, if allowed to display themselves in a more natural setting. For instance, they could be made to sit in anonymity at some selected safe places among the spectators in the stadia and the cameramen asked to focus on them occasionally to catch them in their naturalness.

(A reproduction from the writer's article in 'The Tribune' of 22.5.2013.)

5

IN THE JAT FRATERNITY

Soaked in good natured simplicity and rustic wisdom

72. THE MILK OF HER KINDNESS

Simplicity and openness fascinate me. Way back in 1956, I resigned the job of an auditor under the Punjab Government and came to Delhi to start afresh. Delhi was then a highly livable city, with plenty of open spaces dotted with villages. These places have since filled up to the brim and now look like a honey-comb.

In between the refugee colonies of Malviya Nagar and Kalkaji, there was just the village of Chirag Delhi and the complex of what is now known as the Videsh Sanchar Nigam Ltd. Passing by the centuries old monuments—tombs, mosques, haveli's (old mansions) and palaces— through abundant sunshine and whistling winds, one got a feeling that all was well with the God's world. This was the time when the refugees from Pakistan were struggling to settle down and come good in the new land. These people seemed to put faith in the sweat of their brows and there was air of hope in hearts.

I had landed in the capital city with a first class degree against my name and an inborn flair for teaching, but otherwise hardly anything in my pockets. Soon I found a job in a private school with the facility to stay in the school premises itself. My meager salary, after a while, got supplemented by income from private coaching. I now had not a worry on the Earth.

I could now afford to rent a 'kothari' (a single room accommodation) in Chirag Delhi and live independently. I was to spend some of the best days of my life in this modest accommodation. The village of Chirag Delhi is located in an abandoned fort which has got quite a history of its own. In fact, every square inch of Delhi is soaked in history. From my room, I could see the villagers going to their farms with ploughs on their shoulders and their bullocks in front. On their way back, they had bundles of 'chara' (fodder) on their heads. They hardly passed by me without exchanging a word or two with me—mostly 'Ram Ram, Master'. For some reason, I was a much liked person in the village.

Though I envied the village folk for their simplicity, rustic wisdom, generosity and warmth, they seemed to think that I lived life on a higher plane and was a sort of good influence on their children. If anybody ever tried to be rude or abrasive with me, any number of villagers was instinctively ready to take up cudgels on my behalf. The village appeared to have owned me completely.

A village milkman supplied me a 'pao' (quarter seer) of milk in the morning. Whenever he was not able to bring pure milk for me and had to supply me the 'chalu' milk that he routinely sold to others, he would truthfully declare, "Aaj doodh mein pani sae, Master" (Today, the milk is mixed with water, Teacher). When such declarations became too frequent, I enquired of my land-lady, if she could provide me a quarter seer of milk daily.

When at the end of the month, I went to pay her twelve rupees and eight annas— five towards rent and seven and a half for milk— she refused to accept money for the milk, saying that I was no different from her youngest son, Lal Singh. The gesture touched me deep inside. The milk of her kindness could surely not be paid for in money.

(A reproduction from the writer's article in 'The Hindustan Times' of 14.12.1998.)

73. AN ABRAISIVE TOUNGE, BUT A HEART OF GOLD

With my army, police and legal background, I am perhaps a little too law-abiding for the comfort of some segments of my countrymen. Once while driving my Maruti in New Delhi close to an intersection, I saw the traffic lights turning orange. So, I brought the vehicle to a halt at the stop line. The driver of a Haryana Roadways bus following me closely, however, had different ideas. He felt that there was enough time to cross before the light turned red and found me blocking his way. In this confusion, his bus hit me from behind, giving me quite some jerk and damaging my car slightly.

Far from being apologetic, the driver and the conductor of the bus jumped out and were promptly on me, with their abrasive tongues lashing in full flow. I quietly told them that matter could neither be decided by them nor by me, and both of us had to wait for the police to cover the accident. A PCR van on patrol happened to pass by us. I signaled it to stop and introduced myself to the ASI in charge as a retired police officer. He compulsively came to attention and saluted. This made the driver and the conductor mellow down instantly.

A wireless message was sent to the local police post. A head constable, also a Haryanvi, appeared on the scene on a motorcycle. The now jittery bus driver tried to plead his case with him weakly. The head constable confronted him in his own lingo, "Abbe, seedha aage- peechhe ka case sae, bakwas karan lag reha sae" (You are talking rubbish. It is a straightforward case of your vehicle hitting from behind).

Finally, all of us landed in the police post. The head constable told me matter-of-factly that a charge-sheet against the bus driver would definitely get filed, if I so desired and he was also likely to get punished by the court. However, I shall also have to take the trouble of appearing in the court twice or thrice. I understood all this well, but wanted the bus driver to at least realise his mistake. At this, both the driver and the conductor apologised in unison. Satisfied with this, I started walking back towards my car.

Euphoric over what they perceived as my magnanimity, they came running behind me breathlessly and insisted that I should give them an opportunity to express their gratefulness. They rushed to a nearby shop and brought a dozen bottles of soft drinks, keeping in mind the personnel on duty in the outpost also. The head constable opened one bottle and offered it to me, cleaning its top respectfully with his visibly dirty hankie. He waited for me to finish and asked if I would like to have another one. After I politely declined, he counted the bottles and his staff. One bottle was found surplus. He handed it over generously to the driver and the conductor to share it.

I went away feeling that these people were abrasive of tongue alright, but they, otherwise, had a heart of gold.

(A reproduction from the writer's article in 'The Tribune' of 30.11.2011.)

6

LIFE, AS IT IS LIVED

Life, a gift that directly descends from God

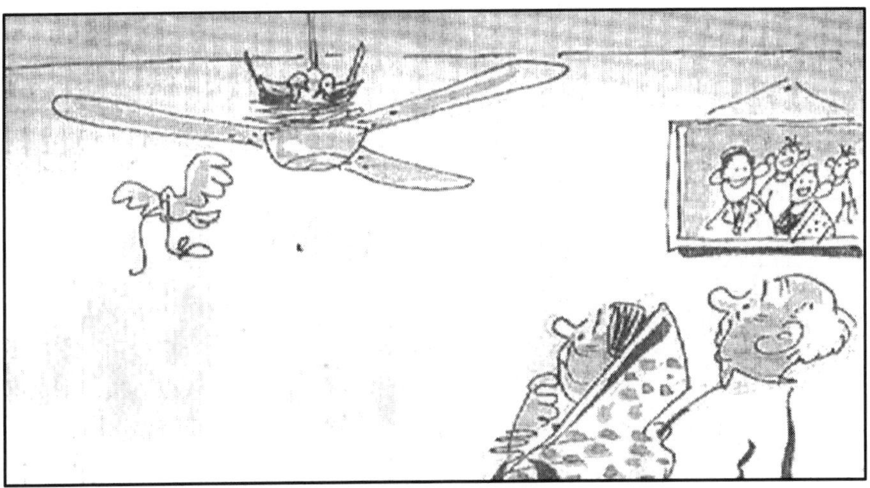

74. IN THE NATURE OF THINGS

Our first light of friendship was lit at Lahore by my uncle, Sh. P.S. Verma. The two families moved so close that we started behaving as kin. After the Partition, our two family friends, Sh. Tilak Ram and Sh. Babu Ram, settled at Delhi. The elder one of them was older than my father. So, we, the children, addressed him as Tayaji.

Tayaji had lost an eye to small pox, which had also left some ugly dots on his face. Very few took note of his helpful nature and his heart of gold. The world goes for appearances. So, people mostly took note of the ugliness of his face and that was perhaps the reason that he could not marry.

Unlike him, his younger brother was a lot more presentable and could even be described as handsome. He married and raised a family of around a dozen children. The poor soul appeared to live only to earn for them and his devoted wife, to just rear them. I wonder if they ever had time to think of themselves. They must have, however, dreamt that their abundant progeny would at least ensure a secure and decent old age for them. They would thus make up for all that they had lost in the prime of their life.

At long last, their eldest son grew up, did his B.Tech from one of our I.I's.T and after an agonizing wait at home, got a decent job for himself. It was now time for him to get married and he did. I stop the story here to pick the threads of another that would help to understand life, as it is lived in its natural course.

We then lived in a spacious flat in R.K.Puram at New Delhi—open, well-lit and windy. We had a liking for a tomb-like openness and thus, mostly kept the windows open. This was an invitation to a couple of turtle-doves to set up their nest on the top shelf of one of our open almirahs. They brought lot of straw for the nest and shed quite a few unwanted feathers that kept our floor awfully dirty. Once or twice we cleaned up their nest to drive them out. But the tenacious birds just would not leave the place. Finally, some lingering softness in our hearts made us yield before their persistence.

Soon we could see two tiny eggs in the nest and then hear the chirping of their offspring.The dutiful parents were seen bringing worms and other food and the young ones raising their beaks greedily to receive their bite. The lazy young fellows seemed happy being fed this way in the nest, but this was too good to last forever. The parent birds soon started coaxing the reluctant fellows out of their nest. Their pathetic protests that it was too early for this were ignored and they were put on a training course for flying and fending for themselves straight away. One of the young fellows, while being forced out of the nest, fluttered its wings angrily for a while and then fell on the floor in a thud amid woeful cacophony. The ruthless parents, however, did not find it funny and displayed their noisy disapproval at this malingering in no uncertain terms.

Finally, both the little rogues descended on to the window, had a good look at the world outside and perhaps liked it. They flew out never to return again. The parent birds were sad. The nest remained silent for a long while. However, having done their duty by the nature, they also flew out to some place to disintegrate into eternity— nobody has perhaps seen any bird dying a natural death. Unlike us, the humans, they do not expect their young ones to look after them in their old age. In their case, it is just a one-way traffic.

I now come back to the earlier story. We happened to visit our Tayaji's place a few years later. Our aunt (wife of his younger brother) appeared to be struggling to look serene and labouring to hide her hurt. When we enquired about her eldest son, we learnt that he had set up a separate home with his wife and rarely came to visit them. The silent sadness of the lady gored our heart and left us thinking whether we, like the lesser creatures of nature, should just reconcile to the fact that the life-cycle is just a one-way duty by nature or we are really on a higher plane and have a right to expect our progeny to give something back to us in the sunset of our lives.

(A reproduction from the writer's article in 'The Pioneer' of 24.7.1999.)

75. THE RETIREMENT BLUES

Weary and burdened with their work routine, people often look forward to their day of retirement. But once there, different sort of ideas engulf them. For one, they think that the things would never be the same again. Having enjoyed some kind of institutional support for years, one now feels weak and vulnerable. Though there is no boss to be bothered about, nobody has to really bother about you either.

Within the family also, the sudden loss of clout may be a rather uncomfortable feeling. Scheme of the nature is such that nobody ever wants to part with the position of the prime mover or decision-maker. Even your wife may think that you are not fit to be given all the respect and considerations of the bread-winner, though it may still be your pension sustaining the family. After all you do not work anymore. The pension is not deemed to be a deferred wage, but a sort of charity to you. In the absence of interest in something substantial, one may also drift in to a mental state of aimlessness and time may then really hang heavy on the retired person.

Besides, the retirement age in our country is around sixty and the average life span of the Indians also happens to be just a few years above this. Thus, another thought that may trouble one no end is that his end itself after all may not be very far off. However, the average age of about sixty-four is based on the expectancy of life at birth. If somebody has reached the age of sixty in normal health, a different law of averages comes in to play and one may hope to live another fifteen to twenty years. But, this notwithstanding, most of us find it difficult to free ourselves from this fixation of fear.

Nonetheless, one does come across people occasionally for whom the death holds no horrors. They appear to be as much interested in the next world as they are in this one. Take the case of Sant Vinova Bhave who renounced the body as soon as he felt that it was no longer suitable to lodge his soul. Sarmad, a sufi of the Aurangzeb era, was sentenced to execution as a heretic for moving about naked. The saintly man saw his God in the executioner's sword and kissed it saying that he would not fail to see Him in whatever form he cared to come to take him.

I also happened to meet a godly soul who seemed to see Rama in his wrinkles. Frail figure of a man in his eighties, he had his own share of old-age ailments. He never asked anybody to do anything about these. In fact, he had stopped entertaining any worldly worries long time back and always wore a look of serenity about his being. Whenever, I enquired of him about his well being, his face would light up and with the eagerness of a child about to be taken to Disneyland and he would say that he was sitting in all readiness for the divine call.

On the final night of his worldly existence, his son who had got up for the toilet, found him lying on the floor. He thought that his father might have fallen from the cot. He picked him up tenderly and put him back on the bed. He then left him dozing in peace. In the morning the saintly man was again found lying on the floor— lifeless this time. (Dying on the bed is, of course, considered inauspicious in our belief system). Obviously, the pious old man had a clear premonition about his end and was amply prepared for it. He deservedly died a death that many would envy.

However, the best way to overcome the retirement blues for ordinary mortals like us is not to retire ever. The U.S. Supreme Court judges, Field Marshalls, advocates, politicians etc never retire. All of us could not be one of them, but we could always keep ourselves engaged in something meaningful all through and die with our boots on.

(A reproduction from the writer's article in 'The Pioneer' of 24. 8.1998.)

76. JUST NEXT TO GOD

All life comes directly from God, but, next to God, mother is the most important agent of the procreative process of nature. Superficially, it would appear that life originates in a male body. The sperms that it produces in gay abundance are the living organisms and they make an energetic effort of their own to get to the ovum waiting in the fallopian tube of the female. The ovum, on the other hand appears to be an inert object, flowing effortlessly in the body fluids and getting guided by muscular spasms and suction processes. Medical science, however, asserts that woman can bring a female life in to being of her own, though she is incapable of bearing male offspring in the absence of the 'X' chromosome in her body.

All this notwithstanding, male role in the process ends as quickly as it begins. After the sperms are released in her body and an odd one among these happens to fertilize her ovum, it is the mother whose body undergoes all the ordeal of bringing a proper life in to the world. In fact, the intensity of relationship between the mother and her baby continues well after the bearing stage and birth. There is certainly something unearthly about this bond. A mother, whose child had got stuck under the wheels of a truck, thought that she needed to lift the vehicle a little to rescue her child. In this super human effort, she had to summon the very last bit of strength from her sinews and the extreme stress cracked a few of her ribs. She, however, did manage to retrieve her child.

What to speak of a human mother, a female pig was seen doing something similar in Nagaland during my tenure there. Its owners had decided to slaughter it for a celebration in the family that evening. They had a gun alright, but they wanted to save on the cartridge. So they tried to kill her by giving heavy blows on the head with a log of wood. But despite the blows it kept on running here and there. So they finally decided to fetch the gun from inside. Meanwhile, even in that state of breathlessness, with blood profusely flowing from its mouth, the disoriented mother came running to its pig lings out of its concern for their safety and tried to hide them by putting straw on these with her blood stained mouth. Again, I saw a puppy over-run by a vehicle surrounded by its mother and siblings. It was in a hopeless condition with its own flesh pushed into its mouth from within. Still, the mother licked it for hours in an effort to bring it back to life.

I witnessed something of this nature yet again when I went to file my income-tax return at 'Mayur Bhawan' at New Delhi quite a few years back. I was accompanied by my son, Ajay, who is a paediatrician by profession and was recently blessed with a son himself. His wife, Sakshi also happens to be child-specialist. During the course of their training and also their stint as consultants, they must have already saved scores of budding lives. It is, in fact, the likes of them who have brought the expectancy of life in the country to near about the world standards. They, thus, have a particular sensitivity towards nascent lives struggling for survival. The babies who got a new lease of life at their hands, of course, would not remember it but their mothers would certainly not be able to forget them.

I must say that the income-tax people had made all arrangements to make life easy for thousands of assessees who thronged the halls to file their returns. However, they could not do much about the weather that had decided to be particularly atrocious on that day. The atmosphere in the crowded halls was, indeed, unbearably stuffy. Yet, nobody was complaining as the income-tax officials were dutifully there to share all the steamy discomforts of the place with the milling crowds.

When we came out after filing our income-tax returns, we found a female monkey perched on a wall of the building and holding dirty looking something close to its heart. It seemed to have completely forgotten about the usual playfulness in its blood and sat still, solemn and sad, just throwing a look around at the crowds. My son pointed my attention to it and wished that he had a camera with him. I thought the point of his interest possibly was the very simian presence in the complex, as if it was also keen to file its income-tax return in time. But, no, my son explained that what it was holding by its heart was a few months old mummified body of its baby. It was still reluctant to part with it and appeared to be on the look-out for a messiah in the large crowd who would somehow bring it back to life with some sort of a magic touch.

So, all mothers are made that way inside.

(A reproduction from the writer's article in 'The Tribune' of 21.7.2004.)

77. THE LANGUAGE OF LIFE

During my long service with the government, I have attended a number of computer courses on system design and analysis with the Computer Maintenance Corporation, Crimes Record Bureau and my own organisation i.e. the C.R.P. Force. With my background of mathematics, I did quite well in all these programmes. However, I still feel that I am not adequately literate in computers.

Occasionally, I take the help of my grandson, yet to be seven, when I get stranded on my personal computer. His principal area of interest is, of course, the video games. But he often ensures that my computer gets in a mood to comply with my commands also.

However, while struggling to learn computers, I strayed on to a bit of philosophy. I picked up a realisation that the binary language of the computer is symbolic of the language of life. Computer is based on the inter-play of eight tiny bulbs. These get individually lighted or go off on command to permute into 256 combinations that have been assigned various characters like the digits from 0 to 9, letters of various languages and mathematic symbols etc. These characters and their combinations are used to give commands to the computer that is programmed to respond to these.

Coming now to life, the scheme is strikingly similar. Human brain is some sort of a super computer, having a C.P.U. with a high-class computing ability and a gigantic R.A.M. in the form of a highly complex memory disc. Our senses that provide inputs to the brain act like the key board and our thoughts as monitors. We could see some sort of a binary system operating in our lives also. Some of us are good (a lighted bulb) and some are bad (a bulb that is off) — of course, the good means more good than bad and the bad is more bad than good. Some promote love and others hatred, some inflict wounds on the humanity and the others strive to heal these, some create wealth and the others destroy it, some earn through the sweat of their brows and others feed on their effort, some look highly presentable and some ungainly. One could go on like this to eternity. So let us conclude here that some of us are positively bestowed and some are negatively charged.

What then is the sum total of everything? Do the things just cancel each other out into an ultimate nothingness? No, though the material remains the same it constantly keeps changing shape. Thus, iron ore gets converted into a Swiss watch, allied with alumina it metamorphoses in to an aircraft; fossils become a valuable source of energy and so on. The world today is a lot different from the lump of the gases that somehow got cast away from the Sun billions of years back.

Thus, the binary aspect of life, though a universal phenomenon, is not all that is to a life. The essential difference is that there are shades of grey in life that a computer does not cater for.

(A reproduction from the writer's article in 'The Tribune' of

78. RISING ABOVE BLOOD

I have been a keen student of history, which largely is an account of the high and mighty. I have read about many majestic mortals, but even they often failed to rise above their blood. Whenever it came to doing justice where their own kin were involved, they were not able to live up to their high reputations and rather, more often than not, badly floundered.

All of us know a lot about the greatness of Emperor Akbar. But when it came to his own rebellious son, Saleem, he proved to be just a father. This erratic son had openly rebelled twice against the state. The common rebels were routinely put to death. Saleem, however, being his father's son, escaped with just a few slaps on his face and solitary confinement for a few days. After this, when he was produced before the emperor wearing a few days old stubs and looking miserable, the father in the emperor just melted like wax. History now knows this errant son as Shehanshah Jehangir!

Jehangir, in turn, became famous for his legendary sense of justice. Ironically, it is again a fact of history that he also let his rebellious son, Khusrao, escape with the punishment of blinding while he was made to pass through a pathway in Agra, astride which the bodies of his fellow rebels were exhibited impaled on spears. Even his punishment of blinding was executed in a manner that his eye sight could be partially restored at a later stage. Guru Arjun Dev, who just blessed Khusrao, as he had been routinely doing in case of all his faithful, was tortured to death.

Years back, I read an article in a newspaper that questioned the very existence of Rani Padmini of Chittor, who is a sort of our national heroine. Stung by this belated claim, I decided to investigate the truth about her. I even left my government job to do justice to my research project. After spending around twenty-five years on the subject, I was able to piece together enough evidence to conclude that the celebrated queen does not sit on our national psyche just for nothing. She is very much an illustrious persona of our history and did commit jauhar at Chittor in 1303 AD. We can really be proud of her sense of virtue, valour, wisdom and of course, her unworldly beauty.

One side benefit of my extensive study has been the exploration of history stretching to a period of over five hundred years before and after Padmini. During this period, some amazing incidents of proven historicity came to my notice. In 1302 AD, during the seize of the Ranthambhor fort by Alauddin Khalji, Raja Hamir Dev Chauhan's garrison inside was driven to a situation where the Rajputs traditionally flung open the gates for the last ditch battle with the enemy, while their ladies perished in the fire of 'jauhar'. Some loyal neo-Muslims, like Mohammad Shaw Kameezi (fondly referred to as Mahima Sahi in a near contemporary Sanskrit work), were then in the service of the Chauhan ruler. The Maharaja thought that he had no right to expect them to die in the manner of the Rajputs. So he offered to evacuate Kameezi and his companions from the fort about to fall. Stung inside, Kameezi maintained his composure and requested the Maharaja to come to his 'haveli', as his wife wanted to express her gratitude before they left. The ruler granted his wish. As he entered Kameezi's mansion, he was aghast to see that the loyal soldier had killed his entire family— a Muslim's version of 'jauhar'. The ruler now had no choice but to extend the honour of joining the suicidal mission to Kameezi and his companions. Even Alauddin was deeply moved by the sight of the hero fallen by the side of his master and ordered a decent burial for him.

The other case of a person rising above the blood is that of Panna Dhai. She had her infant son killed to save the life of the future ruler of Mewar, Maharana Udai Singh. My search for the truth about Padmini took me to many places and persons. One such man was the Dhai Bhai of the present Maharana of Mewar. The clout that this grand old man enjoyed in the royal family was to be seen to be believed and why not— he after all was a being of the world where people did things that many would envy, but few dare.

(A reproduction from the writer's article in 'The Hindustan Times' of 28.9.2000.)

79. NOTHING TO HIDE

This is a story from my childhood at Lahore, when I was just about six years old. My father got me admitted to the second standard in Dev Samaj School, close to our residence in Vasant Nagar. My mother got me bathed every morning, applied generous amount of mustard oil on my head and rubbed it hard. She then took care to pour two 'gadbi`s' (a narrow-necked brass pot) of water over me to ensure that the superfluous oil got washed away.

There was nothing like school uniform in our institution those days. Most of us went to the school dressed in 'kurta' (shirt) and 'churidar' pajama, tight-fitting at the ankles end, but baggy over the buttocks. More fashionable ones came in 'neekar' (half-pant) with their shirt tucked into it. Some Muslim boys attended school dressed in 'choga`s' (long shirts). At least one of them, Badr-u-slam, wore nothing under his 'choga'.

Corporal punishment by 'ustad`s' (teachers) was quite a routine those days and the most usual way of chastising was to make the pupils sit in the 'murga' (chick) position for half an hour or so. This posture was assumed by squatting and passing hands through the thighs and calf muscles from behind and holding the ears. To add to their discomfort, they were periodically warned not to droop, but keep their buttocks up. The raised buttocks sometimes got thrashed with a cane.

The teachers, in turn, used to be terribly afraid of the Inspector of Schools. His periodic visits put the teaching staff, including the Head Master, in lot of tension. They did all in their power to ensure that the inspector went holding a high opinion about their performance, the main ingredient of which was, of course the proficiency of their pupils. During one such supervisory visit, our class teacher, Abdul Hakim, thought of a rather innovative plan to hoodwink the inspector. He made us sit in tidy rows in such an order as would ensure that every weak student had a bright one behind him to enable him to copy.

I, thus, had Badr-u-slam in front of me. I solved the arithmetical sum given to us correctly and duly slipped my slate to the front on the sly for Badru to copy. But 'nakal' (copying) also involves certain amount of 'akal' (intelligence) which, unfortunately, my this friend seemed to be totally lacking. So, he failed to copy correctly to the great annoyance of our teacher. After the inspector was gone, he promptly made Badru assume the 'murga' position while I also got a few slaps. With Badru not wearing any underwear as usual, what a sight he was in front of me!

After many years, I heard that once Charles de Gaulle, the president of the provisional government of France, went to call on Winston Churchill in his hotel suite. When he entered after giving the courtesy knock on the door, he was taken aback and tried to withdraw in a hurry. Churchill, sitting in his birth day suit, however, beckoned him to come right in, saying that the Prime Minister of England had nothing to hide from the President of France. The joke instantly brought the memories of Badru in 'murga' position flashing before me.

(A reproduction from the writer's article in 'The Tribune' on 19.2.2013.)

80. IN THE QUEUE

Quite a few pearls of wisdom lie scattered in the Shakespearian writings. One among these is, "Apparel oft proclaims the man". In the same flow, I would say that queues also often declare the civilisational status of a place. More patient and peaceful the queues, more orderly would be the lifestyle of the people around.

This idea regarding queues being related to quality of life got cultured in my mind spontaneously while standing in a queue before a reservation counter at the Delhi Cantonment railway station recently. The first demoralising element was the very length of the line. Then it was moving at a snail's pace. At least, that is what we in the queue felt. To top it all, the constant chants of, "Bhai sahib line mein aeyey (come in the line, brother)" was another irritant.

Nevertheless, however irritated and exasperated they felt inside, most of the people in the queue were at least keeping their outer calm and quiet grace. Gone were the days when the people got into quarrels at the drop of a hat. A trip in Delhi's Metro would perhaps further strengthen this feeling.

As the time went by slowly, even the small little things started registering in my mind. Some people perhaps do not like to be seen standing with the common folk in the queue. They, thus, have a tendency to stand to a side, giving rise to the risk of another queue forming behind them. If a lady is there in the line, the man behind likes to leave a sizeable gap in between and a bulky man, in any case, makes the queue look longer than it is. Thus, when a lady or a big man or a man standing to a side got served, there was an air of inexplicable relief in the queue.

Amid all this, we kept inching our way to the window. Just when it was my turn for the ticket, the booking clerk got up and walked away leaving us marooned. There were murmurs of discontent all round, though we knew the man must have gone on a short trip to the toilet. How we wished that he had been provided a commode underneath himself in lieu of the chair. Mercifully, to our great relief, he was back without taking much time.

At long last, I got my tickets and left the window, but not before throwing a look of pity for the people still in the queue.

(A reproduction from the writer's article in 'The Tribune on 31.5.2006.)

81. A BRUSH WITH THE ISLAMIC LAWS

LAST year, my near and dear ones serving in Saudi Arabia got in trouble at the hands of their Muslim maid. They had got this girl from Bangladesh under their sponsorship. The maid was excessively ambitious. As the settled salary did not satisfy her, she quickly established contacts with some Bangladesh boys employed in the area to help her find a more lucrative job. She knew quite well that any liaison by a female with unrelated males could have serious implications in the land.

Thus, once when she was under the risk of being discovered in male company (as the door of the flat had accidentally closed on her) she, in her desperation, climbed on to the roof and jumped in the balcony. The hard landing broke a few of her vertebrae.

Her sponsors promptly arranged for her surgery though it involved quite some cost. However, rather than being grateful, the wily woman started getting ideas on way to her recovery. Finally, she came up with an allegation that she had, in fact, been pushed down the stairs by her employers. Obviously, she thought that this threat of criminal action would enable her to milk maximum money out of them.

In the circumstances, the Saudi police got involved in the matter. Fortunately, some neighbours had seen the employer couple leaving for their duties minutes before the mishap. Additionally, there was proper record of their presence at their places of duty. The Muslim witnesses upheld the truth despite the accused being Hindus. They said that Allah, above everything else was truth and they had to stand by the innocent couple.

Unlike in India, the Saudi police enjoy the confidence of law. The statements recorded by them are taken to be true, unless proved otherwise. The police after careful investigation exonerated the couple. Still, the law had to take its own Saudi Arabian course. Thus, the matter finally landed with their "Sheikh", the counterpart of our Sessions Judge. Our lawyers are conversant with the Islamic law, as it forms part of our legal history. So, I was requested to come and help as a lawyer.

The police officers whom I met were extremely courteous. The investigating officer always took care to visit us in civil dress and in his private car, so as not to cause any embarrassment to us in our neighbourhood. The judiciary, once being convinced of our innocence, was all the more decent and helpful. Finally, the case was sorted out with due human touch all around. Not only the honour of the couple was fully restored but also their humane approach in the face of provocation was appreciated.

Many may consider the Islamic laws out of tune with the times today. However, more than the language of the laws, it is their interpretation and implementation that is of prime essence.

(A reproduction from the writer's article in 'The Tribune' of

82. HIS MAJESTY—THE COMMON MAN

I am proud of my high status as a common man. The high and mighty come to me and cajole me for my vote. Even in the ethos of dictatorship, I have the takers. The dictators look to me for legitimacy and resort to referendums to make it appear that they have my mandate to rule. I do understand that nobody's heart really bleeds for me and the political concern for me is only election-deep. In fact, the politicians just hate me because they find me too demanding. Still, they do not have any option, but to woo me. Anybody who wants to be somebody—rich and famous—understands my importance.

Also, the way I am treated is an indicator of the civilizational level of a country. I am normally a calm and quiet person. But when tormented beyond the limit of my tolerance, I rise like a tornado and then the Louis's get guillotined, Charles's beheaded, Shah's driven out of their domains and kings, emperors, Czars, Presidents, Prime Ministers and their governments made to lick dust. In fact, that is the defining hour when I wake one morning and find myself famous.

Curiously, despite all my importance, nobody disturbs me during my walks, my visits to restaurants, my shopping stints and so on. Nobody has to give excuses on my telephone that I am busy in a meeting or just not there. I do not have to be afraid of any paparazzo stalking me. Should I even be one day caught with my pants down, I am sure, the people would just like to look the other way. How silly of me that, for a long while, I thought of my journey on retirement from a commanding officer to a commoner as a climb-down!

All sorts of salesmen and showmen of the world have nightmares when they fail to attract my attention. The whole world seems to be out to pamper me. Films are shot, songs composed, TV serials produced and columns are written keeping me in mind. I do not have much to give to anybody, but still many are after me with their attractive offers, promotion schemes, rewards and incentives. What is it really that these people want from me — my little money, my mandate, my admiration, my adulation, my adoration or what?

Even the newspapermen come to my door to persuade me to buy their papers. So as a reader or as a viewer, I can afford to nurse high ideas. I can just refuse to read even the biggest of the names or view anything that is so fondly put on the screen for my benefit.

The trouble starts when I try to be a writer myself or want to see myself on the screen. Then, I painfully learn how scarce is the space in the columns and how flush the channels are with material. All the celebrities of the world are my creation. I often produce them out of nothing. Sadly, however, I invariably lose out when I try to be something myself.

(A reproduction from the writer's article in 'The Tribune' on 12.4.2004.)

83. WIVES, WORLD OVER

I have now been a government pensioner for around twenty-four years. On many occasions, I have tried to convince my wife that pension is a sort of deferred wage and thus, my pension is, in fact, a payment for my past hard work. She, however, thinks that all this is bunkum and for a long while now, I have been used to living on an unemployment dole. She has given me a feeling that all wives want their husbands doing some job all through their lives and return home in the evening exhausted. Then, of course, they may bring them some comfort by running around them with a glass of water and a cup of tea. And as they settle down, they may also be made to believe that they were missed by them all the day long. The fact, however, is nobody wants a boss to breathe down his neck all the time.

My perpetual presence by my wife is not the only problem between us. She also feels that I have somehow managed to break free of my responsibilities, while she still has to slave around at home. When I plead with her that I write three to four articles every month, she is not impressed. She would, in fact, never agree that those who write also work. Her retort is that I would have earned much more for the family, if I had chosen to do some worthwhile work and now even my erstwhile orderlies earned more than me. She is particularly unhappy over the fact that normal people look for extensions or other avenues of fruitful work after retirement, while I had left my lucrative job many years before superannuation, ostensibly to do creative work.

She is unprepared to believe that my pension is an earned income. As for my writing, she insists that the general idea behind it is merely to kill time, as she herself does by playing rummy and participating in kitty parties. We often conclude our case against each other, with her insistence that I am wasting my time by doing something worthless and I maintaining, rather unkindly, that what I am doing is beyond the understanding of the likes of her.

Her more serious complaint is that I need something to eat every two hours during the day, a sure sign of a man without work— as the Punjabi saying goes "Vehleh bandey da chulahey kanni dhyan" (A person without work is always looking to what is being cooked on the hearth). I counter her by quoting the case of Sultan Mahmud Begarha of Gujarat (1458-1511 AD) who needed something to eat all through the night even and that too while he was still working. History knows the man as a great glutton. He would have bowls of 'biryani' placed on both sides of his bed when he retired for the day. And whichever side his sleep got disturbed, he would start helping himself from the bowl kept on that side. He often said good-naturedly, "Who would have fed Mahmud, had he not been the king"? This historical support wins the argument for me. Rather, the busy lady fears that otherwise I would waste some more of her time by reading from the history books kept on my study table. While withdrawing from the scene, she does not, however, fail to naughtily mutter, "You are no different from, what you said of King Bekara". I protest, "Begarha not Bekara".

But, she reluctantly concedes that I after all may not be the most ease-loving and food-loving person in this wide world. The very next second, however, she topples me again with a soulful sigh, "How I wish that I could also retire like you!" All said, between the two us we have a talking point that is sure to last a life time.

(A reproduction from the writer's article in "The Hindustan Times' of 13.12.1999.)

84. IN SEARCH OF IDEAS

I suspect that all people secretly hold a high opinion about their intelligence and abilities. Some, of course, make no secret of what they think they are. Quite a few, both high and low, entertaining exaggerated ideas in the area of writing walk into the editorial offices with wads of paper in their hands, hoping to enlighten the world with their views.

This, however, is hardly the place for all dreams to come true, as I have myself learnt through experience. The space in the columns is just too scarce and precious for everyone to be there. There is hardly a doubt in my mind that reader is the King. Nobody can make him read what he does not want to. He can thus afford to disregard biggest of the names in the business of writing. Many budding writers go back wondering why, in the first place, they thought of lowering their high profile as readers by wanting to be writers. Many others who fail to shoot the bull in the first attempt leave the place with the look of an army general who thinks he has lost only a battle and not the war. They often make a come-back.

Being one of such bug-bitten writers, I also keep paying visits to the editorial offices— after all, mountain does not come to Mohammad; Mohammad has to go to the mountain. I have seen many interesting things happening there and this one is the typical. An old gentleman, wanting to give the benefit of his views to the world, had sent a piece to a newspaper office around a month back. Normally, it should have come back to him along with the editor's compliments in about a week. When this did not happen, a hope was raised in his mind that the contribution might have been retained for possible use.

Thrice he went to the place to find out about the fate of his article and every time the secretary to the editor sent him to the section where his valuable piece was supposedly stuck. His persistence and pestering had by then had driven the matters to such a stage that the exasperated section-in-charge finally asked him to see the editor himself. He came fuming back to the secretary demanding to know who the editor was and where he could be met. I could not help feeling amused. In fact, I felt like telling him that he was sitting just in the adjoining room, wondering why the secretary was holding back this simple truth. Then, however, I realized that the principal job of the secretary was to ensure that too many people did not disturb his boss.

Painstakingly, he rang up many other sections taking time off his normal work. Finally the elusive article was located with the dispatch section. It was duly marked for return. The secretary had it brought to him and he, in turn, handed it over to the indignant man with a sigh of relief. Before moving out, however, he did not fail to make a last ditch effort, "Since you say that you have not seen it, shall I leave it with you?" It took the secretary another ten minutes to convince him that the concerned assistant editor had read it and no purpose would be served, if he left the piece with him.

Now, a word about the editors (who are always the writers themselves) would also be in order. Silence and solitude could also be a distraction sometimes. They are thus often seen wandering out of their chambers, as if in some sort of a trance. First, I thought this was their way of keeping an eye on their staff. After all, they, like Admiral Nelson, must also be wanting their newsmen to do their duty. Then, I wondered if they too were curious to know, if anything interesting was going on in their secretariat.

But, after a while I found out that they also have the usual writer's itch and stroll out just in search of ideas and the suitable words to put these in. Perhaps they know the myriads patterns woven in vacuum may miss on many things. Active interaction with life as it is lived, even within the confines of their offices, brings freshness to the columns.

(A reproduction from the writer's article in 'The Pioneer' of 26.6.1998.)

85. MAN OF THE MOUNTAINS

Ever since her marriage to me some 47 years back, my wife had been nostalgic about the areas around the Rohtang La, the Himalayan pass that can now take you all the way to Leh, and from there to Karakoram, Yarkand and Khotan to link up with the legendary 'Silk Road'. During my service in the armed forces, I took her around the entire length and breadth of the country and even abroad. But we somehow missed the Kullu-Manali belt.

My son, Ajay and his wife, Sakshi, were aware about their mother's longing for this valley where she had spent the formative years of her childhood and finally lost her father to the mountains.

Her father, Dr. Brij Lal Laroia had seen service in the most inhospitable parts of the Himalayas like, Skardu (now in P.O.K.), Kargil, Lahaul, Spiti and many places in the Beas valley. He was some sort of Dr. Kotnis for the mountain villages, always on the move to bring succor to these scattered people.

Our children snatched time from their busy schedule as paediatricians to arrange for a trip to Manali that year. It was to be a journey down the memory lane for my wife. On her way, she was keen to locate their wooden house at Bhunter where she had spent her babyhood and still dreamt of the apples, pears and plums heaped in their verandah. Sadly, there was no trace of the building and even the landmarks around. The vast open space where the 'Devtas' (deities from the surrounding villages) used to be brought during the Dusehra festivities was now the Kullu Airport.

On our further drive to Manali, we could see the mountains sprinkled with snow, the rubber rafts being buffeted in the gushing waters of Beas, tall conical trees positioned like ballistic missiles ready to shoot into the skies, hill peaks peeping above the clouds and the greenery spread over the ground in myriad forms. Manali, however, was bustling with vehicles and people many times more than the place could take. In fact, one felt like being in an over-crowded Punjab Roadways bus.

The next day we left for the Rohtang La. We had to stop three kilo metres short, as further ahead vehicles were lined up right up to the 13050 feet high pass. Ajay and I were able to make to the pass wading through snow, converted almost into a dirty mass of mud by the human feet. Sakshi and the kids had to be content with throwing balls of snow at each other at the spot.

My wife, however, sat solemn on a stone by the roadside. She was obviously thinking of her father who, some 52 years back, sat similarly for rest somewhere here after a hard day's trek on duty and froze to death. Manali is known as the 'Valley of gods'. He was no less a god to his patients in the mountain villages around. After all, he lived and died for them.

(A reproduction from the writer's article in 'The Tribune' of 6.6.2007.)

86. THE GREAT SURVIVOR

For years he fought illnesses and crises. Now he is no more. His body has been handed over to the All-India Institute of Medical Sciences, New Delhi, for medical research in accordance with his will. The great survivor thus still lives after death in the cause of humanity. His last wish having been fulfilled, his soul has soared away to the skies with satisfaction while his body would be around in the world for a long while — not in the manner of an Egyptian mummy, looking for the day of its own resurrection, but for the wellbeing of the living.

This noble soul, late Jagdish Jhanji, was half a generation my senior. Well over half a century back, he lost his heart to a lovely young lady in his neighbourhood at Palam Pur and this affair lasted till his death sadly did them apart. Those in love can pick up faintest echoes of affection around them. A few years after his own marriage, he came to know that I was carrying quite a load of love on my heart for his young sister-in-law. He worked furiously behind the scenes to ensure that we got bonded in marriage without fuss. We thus ended up as brothers-in-law and more than that, as soul-mates. Both of us had an identical craze to get into discussion on everything under the sun with anybody around us, whether willing or unwilling for this. Thus, from here onwards we were to share a lot in our heads and hearts.

He spent a good part of his life in the town of Sahnewal in Punjab where his father was a government doctor, enjoying quite some clout in the area. Interestingly, the father of the celebrated film actor, Dharminder, was a school-master at the place and the two were friends. Being socially better placed, Dr Jhanji could afford to act as a big brother with the teacher. When Dharminder decided on a career in the Bollywood, the doctor felt concerned and did not hold back his disapproval for the idea. In fact, one day he asked the school master annoyingly, *"Kiyun pher puttar nu kanjar bana ke hi rehya."* (So, finally you chose to turn your son to the traditional profession of a *"kanjar"*) — the *"kanjar"* tribe in Punjab was then in the profession of singing and dancing that was not considered respectable by the older generation. Dharminder was to later earn the honorific of being the most handsome star of Bollywood and have the privilege of sitting in our Parliament.

Coming back to the main story, Jagdishji had a clear premonition that his end was not very far off. So he got in touch with the Anatomy Department of AIIMS in the Capital and registered himself for the donation of his body. Not being sure, about the reaction of his wife and children to the idea, he left the photo-copies of the documents with me, with a request to see that his last wish was honoured. Still having lingering doubts in mind that worldly attachments might come in the way of his will, he put the document in an amulet which he died wearing.

(A reproduction from the writer's article in 'The Tribune' of 12.1.2012.)

87. LINES OF LOYALTY

When the Indian Cricket League and the Indian Premier League tournaments were launched in our country, I thought that I would have nothing to do with these. Though I myself have been captain of a club level cricket team in Delhi, I often wondered if I had any interest in the proper nuances of the game.

I felt fascinated to cricket merely because this is one sport— a major one at that— where my country counts. The meaningless clash of a few clubs, where there was no scope for taking sides, would, thus, never excite my interest. Soon, however, I found myself sucked in the vortex along with millions, because of the hype created round these meets by the media and money power.

Once there, I learnt to take sides to be able to enjoy the carnivals. After all, Delhi is the place where I live. Rajasthan is the state where my parents lived and died. Punjab is the land of my ancestors where they fought the Mughals by the side of Banda Bairagi and where one of them was to hold the high office of the Diwan of Nabha. A belief also prevails in our family that one of our ancestors paid a huge amount of money to the then fauzdar of Sirhind to obtain bodies of the two 'sahabzada`s' (sons) of the tenth Sikh Guru (who had been laid alive in a wall) to ensure proper performance of their last rites. There was, thus, enough material for my regional sense of loyalty to feed on.

My one wish always is to see that Delhi, Rajasthan and Punjab make it to the play-off stage and then the two among them contest in the finals. I am sure my compatriots from other parts of the country must also be nursing similar obsessions. The lines of loyalty, in fact, run in many directions. We are committed to our countries, communities, clubs and in fact, have many other allegiances too. All these attachments make their own demands on us.

Accordingly, my second wish is that the Indian players should outshine the players of foreign origin all the time. Thus, when Chennai and Bangalore are playing I would likeVinay Kumar to mop up the wickets of Hussy and other foreign players, rather than those of Dhoni and Raina. In fact, the permutations and possibilities in the situation are so many that sometimes I do not really know what exactly I want. This way, however, I manage to keep my interest alive in all the games. I am sure this must be the position with all of us.

Occasionally, rather often, when the things do not move in line with my liking, I put myself at ease thinking that the others also have an equal right to wish the things to go their way. After all, one God is everybody's God and He has to be just and fair to us all.

What, however, really adds to my sense of interest and elation to no end is that those who thought nothing much of our country the other day are now so keen and eager to be part of our show.

(A reproduction from the writer's article in 'The Tribune' of 21.5.2009.)

88. THE BICYCLE AGE

Sometimes after taking the reins of the country, Pt. Jawahar Lal Nehru remarked that India was then passing through the 'Bicycle Age'. At that time 'Hind' and 'Hercules' were the most popular brands of the bicycles in the north India. 'Hind' was lighter and cheaper. It was, therefore, quite popular among the common commuters. 'Hercules' was a sort of workhorse, preferred for its sturdiness by the heavy-duty users like the milkmen. They would hang two to three cans of milk on its carrier and ride around vending milk to the great envy of their poor cousins still selling milk in buckets.

My father was a supervisor with an army ordinance depot at Lahore during the World War II. His office was at quite some distance from Vasant Nagar where we stayed. To overcome his commuting hassles, he finally took one of the most important decisions of his life i.e. the purchase of a bicycle. He would neatly fold the right leg of his trousers and clip it, so that it would not get entangled in the chain and get messed up with greese. He then looked wearing trousers in one leg and a 'churidar pyjama' in the other. After reaching his office, he would take some time off in straightening the folds, so as to give himself a dainty 'babu-like' look.

We withdrew from Lahore before the horrors of the Partition climaxed. My father got a posting at Jaitu, a small marketing town of the princely state of Nabha. Meanwhile, I had also grown up enough to have some fun on our cycle. In my attempt to ride it, I would put one foot on the left pedal and push the other leg through its frame to reach the right pedal, of course, after giving it some speed by hitting the ground hard repeatedly with my right foot. Thus, I rode the bicycle, in what was then called the 'Kainchi' (scissors) style.

Once riding high on confidence, I took the bike on a crowded road. A six-footer 'Khalsa'(Sikh farmer) came right in my way when I was quite at speed. In the confusion, I forgot to apply brakes and instead belatedly rang the bell. The sturdy man first gave me a furious look—I had not only jammed the cycle into his legs from behind, but also had rung the bell to add insult to his injury. However, seeing an apologetic and innocent look at my face, he resisted the idea of giving me a few slaps. The good-natured man instead just went his way looking amused.

The utility bicycles of yester years are well on their way out now. It is mostly some blue-collared workers who are seen commuting on these in some industrial areas. Some children and fitness fanatics are also occasionally seen riding on their designer bikes these days. Otherwise, the 'Bicycle Age' of Nehru`s times is, for sure, over. We are now passing through the age of motor-bikes, if not the motor cars already.

(A reproduction from the writer's article in 'The Tribune' of 14.3.2007.)

89. IN THE CITADEL OF ISLAM

Some years back, I had an occasion to spend around three months in Saudi Arabia, the conscience-keeper of Islam. All faiths fascinate me. I am always keen and curious to understand what makes religions such a mighty magnetic force. So, while in the land, I made it a point to go though the holy Quran and some Islamic literature to have an idea about the faith.

What I understood during my brief study was that a Muslim believes that only Allah is worthy of worship and Prophet Mohammad is his messenger. Allah sits on His magnificient throne on the seventh heaven and during the holy month of 'Ramzan', He comes down to the first heaven to have a closer look at His creation. Thus, the Muslims are advised to be at their best during this period. They are also told that Allah does not have any consort and is all by Himself. There is, therefore, no question of His having any children. They do believe Jesus to be born of the divine will and not through the normal procreative procedure, involving masculine intervention. However, they do not admit him to be the son of God. According to Islam, Allah does not share divinity with anybody. He is, thus, in a sort of master slave relationship with man.

Some local intellectuals invited me for a discussion on religion. Many of them had beards really thick and long, but still they seemed to have open minds. They began with the recitation of a few verses from the Quran which I listened to with respect and reverence, as if I was one of them. After all, they were then in communion with our common Creator.

At the end of this, some of them confronted me with their favourite question: whether Hinduism, with belief in the worship of countless things— planets, plants, animal and stones etc and without any clear-cut concept of God— was a religion? I first referred the questioners to Amir Khusrao's 'Nuh Sipihr' (Nine Heavens) written some seven hundred years back. The celebrated scholar has clarified in his work that the Hindus do worship cattle (cow), plants (basil) and stones etc., but only as His creation and not as God. After all, all life comes directly from Him and in fact, every atom bears His signatures. Every Hindu prayer is, thus, directed to the same divine reality that Muslim call Allah and Hindus by numerous names of their own. Thus, their idolatry has a character entirely different from the one frowned upon by Prophet Mohammad which related to the worship of the idols kept around 'Kaaba' in Mecca as God itself.

Secondly, I suggested to them to visit one of our 'Kumbh Melas' where the largest mass of humanity anywhere on Earth congregates. When they see millions of faces there lit with the same light that they see on the faces of the Hajj pilgrims, they would not ask this question again. They seemed to agree and in fact, had the magnanimity to apologise, if they had in any way hurt my feelings.

(A reproduction from the writer's article in 'The Tribune' of 18.5.2007.)

90. THE HUMAN FEMALE

For ages woman has been loved as a daughter, respected as a wife and worshipped as a mother. However, her tragedy is that when she is not something of man, she is nothing. She has been in demand both as a 'Pativrata' and a prostitute, but sadly not as a person. As beloved of man she could 'launch a thousand ships and burn the topless towers of Ilium'. By herself, she has been weak and vulnerable. Though the things have been improving for her gradually for a century and a half, the change is too slow for her comfort. Her wearing of jeans and mini-skirts, her defiant drinking and smoking and her dancing in the discos etc has not made much difference to her lot. For her, snakes still hiss where the grass is green.

The suffering and subjugation that she has undergone through the ages and the pain that she has swallowed for centuries should be enough to drive any sensitive being to tears. The fact that she has survived all this, is something akin to our subcontinent surviving the slavery of a thousand years and it also seems to confirm the Darwinian doctrine of the 'Survival of the Fittest'. Indeed, she is biologically more stable than the human male—out of around five thousand centenarians in France about a decade back, nearly four thousand were women. Further, as per the recent survey of Gerontology Research Group in the U.S., out of the thirty two oldest persons on earth in June, 2013, thirty one were the females!

Woman is, undoubtedly, the most sophisticated creation of nature. For instance, her body has been provided with three separate orifices at the private space—two for primary excretory functions and one for sex, whereas man has to manage with two and the birds with just one. Man is now largely a sparable for procreation purposes because woman can procreate all by herself (though she cannot deliver male offspring of her own). Again unlike the other female species, she has been endowed with a face and figure matched only by the poetry, paintings and sculptures that these have inspired over the ages.

Then, where does her weakness lie? Of course, woman cannot match man in muscular strength. But, should it really make all this difference? Firstly, it is doubtful if the wrestlers, boxers and weight-lifters have ever ruled this world—men with brains rather than brawn always have. Secondly, law is always there to ensure that the strong do not oppress or overawe the weak. However, within the confines of homes where women live with their men, the law, to a stage, is very reluctant to intervene. This leaves the man in a position of local superiority over his woman at home, as far as muscular strength is concerned. Man has taken full advantage of his superior muscles to hold his woman in bondage over the ages

As an inhuman consequence of this, a quarter of women the world over suffer violent abuse in the privacy of their homes. A recent United Nations survey indicates that this figure could even be as high as 80% in Chile and Pakistan, 60 % in Papua New Guinea, 50% in the Republic of Korea. India itself is not far behind in the matter of this shameful statistics. Only the other day a senior politician from the capital unabashedly admitted in a television interview that he had to be often rough with his wife to force her to yield to sex. He was sure that the others did the same.

In fact, there is an additional dimension to this case in our country—the burning of brides for dowry. An effort has been made to deal with this pernicious problem by inserting some drastic provisions in our penal laws, like Section 304B I.P.C. (for dowry deaths) and 498A I.P.C. (for dowry-related cruelty). But the problem lies buried deep in our psyche and minds cannot be washed clean all that easily. Many, in fact, now hold the view that these legal remedies have, on the ground, proved to be worse than the disease itself, as these look like breaking many a home and some whimsical wives, aided by the myopic, and sometimes unscrupulous, families back in their parental homes, are taking undue advantage of these provisions. So much so that the very institution of marriage has become a highly risky venture for the boys and their families. Among the sufferers are the generals, judges and police officers themselves and their near and dear ones.

Reverting now to the original problem, physical delicacy is not the primary reason for the sad plight of woman. It has instead something to do with the societies' excessive obsession with her chastity. A single false step or just a mishap, her body, mind and soul supposedly get polluted for all time to come. Such a 'kulta' (disgraced women) is left only with one solution to her problems—the nearest village well. Chastity is, indeed, something to be highly cherished. The sexual act does not involve baring of the bodies alone, but the entire being. But, why all the burden of virginity should be borne by the poor lady alone?

Superficially perhaps, sex is a messier affair for woman, as it involves her internal organs, causes irreparable rupture of her hymen on the first occasion and the sexual secretions are also left deposited in her. Besides, this may lead to the multifarious problems of the unwanted pregnancy. However, all this should make no difference from the culpability angle. After all, the main sexual organ is the brain. Pollution if any occurs there. Irrefutably, brain is common to both. Yet, societies seem to think that only the woman gets polluted and the man stays pure, though almost always he is the motivator and in some cases, the outright assailant.

I am afraid, so far as woman is concerned, every human society has blood on its hands. A chapter in our 'Brihidaranyaka' Upanishad talks of what preparations a man should make, if he wants a son of particular attributes. After this preparation, he is told to invite his wife to bed. If the poor thing is not in mood, she could first be lured in to it through inducements. If she was still uncooperative, she could be cursed, disgraced and beaten up. Fatwa-e-Alamgiri (A sort of multipurpose code enacted by Emperor Aurangzeb) also decrees that a woman must obey when she is summoned for sex, once she has accepted the offer of 'mehar' (bridal money) from the husband. In Iran, the Islamic judges are said to have issued orders that any young girl sentenced to death must first be raped, since if executed while still a virgin, she would go to heaven. In sub-Saharan Africa, from Sudan to South Africa and from Mali to Mozambique, spousal abuse is at its worst. Some ethnic groups there are told that if a man`s wife dies before she has been bashed up adequately in her life time, the husband should prove his manhood by beating her corpse! The Russian brides were required to present a birch rod to their husbands as part of their trousseau to beat them with at their will. Even in the most enlightened democracy of the world, the United States of America, domestic violence is the biggest single cause of injury to women, accounting for more hospital admissions than rapes, muggings and road accidents put together.

Curiously, law and societies seem to have chosen different direction for themselves on this issue. In law (except under the Islamic codes), fornication is no offence. adultery and rape are the crimes for the men only. Societies, however, ensure that the woman suffers even heavier punishment for all the three. Laws, in fact, always run ahead of the times and these correspond to the idealism that a society is yet to rise to.

All the above, however, does not mean that man is essentially a villain and woman a paragon of virtue—both are just human. In fact, most of the fighting for the women has been done by men only. Lately, the laws have been substantially strengthened to bring succour to her. What is needed is a more rapid social awakening and attitudinal change, so that daughters are not killed in womb, brides are not burnt for dowry and victims of rape are not stigmatized. Conditions need to be created so that a woman is not afraid to walk alone. This would enable her to come out in the open more freely for education, employment and entertainment. Everything would then fall in place for her in course of time.

(A reproduction from the writer's articles in 'The Statesman' of 24.7.1995 and 'The Daily Excelsior' of 1.3.2007)

7

CURIOSITY

The great human urge to know the unknown

91. THE DUNGEONS OF DEATH

Tucked in the recesses of the Tower of London, are 'The London Dungeons'. There you find displayed the medieval torture techniques and the modes of execution. There are always long beelines of visitors, burning with curiosity to get into the place. One wonders what really attracts the crowds to these gory cells and why such a nauseating display should interest the people. Is there a streak of sadism in every bosom? Or it is the intense curiosity, the thrill of violence, awe of authority of one man over the other, the pleasure of seeing the sinner being punished that interests the people so highly.

Whatever be the magnetism at work, the London Dungeons draw swarms of people to have a look at the bodies being lashed, stretched, split, hanged, burnt, boiled, impaled, guillotined and tormented in many other ways. It is undoubtedly the same human instinct that drew the people in droves to witness the battering of buttocks and crushing of kidneys of the so called offenders in Zia-ul-huq's Pakistan. The same impulse is behind the people eagerly waiting to see some criminals being beheaded outside the mosques in Saudi Arabia on Fridays.

Once in after coughing up a good amount of cash, one's mind finds itself in a fast moving lift slipping rapidly into the centuries gone by. What now greets a person is the gloom of the dungeons, contorted and bleeding bodies and shrieks of the tormented beings. The light and sound effects are deftly used to give a ghostly touch to the place. From one of the cells rises the soft and shivering voice of young Mary, the Queen of Scots, as she is taken to the execution block for beheading. With the mixture of a sigh and shriek, the fear-stricken voice announces to the world how badly the poor thing wished to live.

From another cabin comes the voice of Anne Boleyn, the second queen of Henry VIII, pleading her innocence. The luckless lady was executed on allegations of adultery. Her face that had once made the king discard his first wife, the Catherine of Aragon, was now aghast at her wretched fate. She, at her own request, was allowed to be beheaded by an expert swordsman and not by an executioner with his customary axe.

In another dungeon lies the effigy of King Charles I who, after being deposed, was beheaded on January 30, 1649. His head is being sewn back on to his body so that he may be discovered in tact on the day of resurrection. Common criminals condemned to death were, however, not so lucky. They were hung, disemboweled and then quartered i.e. cut into four pieces, each containing a limb. These pieces were then buried in unconsecrated grounds in four corners of the city, so as to render their resurrection impossible! As per an Act passed during the reign of Henry VIII, those guilty of homicide by poisoning were boiled to death.

The dungeons of death could, however, not miss to display the most dreaded beheading machine of the French Revolution, the guillotine. It was invented by Dr, Joseph Ignace Guillotine. The machine was first tested on unclaimed corpses, then on live sheep and calves, before it was cleared for human use. It claimed its first human victim in Nicholas Jacques Pelletier who was executed in April, 1792. The oldest victim to be beheaded was 97 years old Councillor Dupin and the youngest, the 14 year old, Charles Dubosts. Even today the machine sends chill down the spine.

The London Dungeons are quite appropriately located close the Tower Hill and the Tower of London. Tower Hill is the historic spot of public executions. The last man to be beheaded here was Simon, Lord Lohat, way back in 1747 AD. The wooden block used for beheading him is displayed in lower chamber of the Martin Tower in the Tower of London along with some other instruments of torture. In fact, Queen Elizabeth I maintained a private torturer on her establishment who was accommodated in her own palace, the White Tower.

Englishman, indeed, has a keen business sense—it is not for nothing that Napoleon called England a 'Nation of Shopkeepers'. The exit from the London Dungeons is, thus, through a shop selling curios, souvenirs and mementos. A T-shirt on sale here has a painting of an executioner about to wield his axe. He finds that the hands of the convict have also strayed on to the block alongside his head. The executioner cautions the convict to mind his fingers. After all, the kind-hearted man did not believe in inflicting unnecessary violence. His job was just to chop off the head!

(A reproduction from the writer's article in 'The Tribune' of 31.10.1992.)

92. A CLOSE LOOK AT THE GALLOWS

I was around ten when Mahatma Gandhi fell to Godse's bullets with 'Hey Ram' on his lips. Even at that age I wondered at the circuitry of the human brain. After all, how could anybody even think of killing a man who wished everybody well? So, Nathu Ram Godse had to be taken as an arch criminal for assassinating the 'Father of the Nation'. Yet it was also a fact that he did not kill him for any personal gain. You could not treat him as a lunatic either, for he exactly knew what he had done and why. Thus, the history has to record the man as a sort of criminal of conscience.

When I joined the D.A.V. College at Ambala, I strangely felt fascinated by the central jail of the city where Godse was hanged to death. Once, I made up my mind to have a look at this jail. I knew that the jail officials would not allow me inside. If my pleading with them did not work, I shall at least be able to peep in or have a close look at it from outside.

What a luck, the front portion of the jail then happened to be under extensive repairs and the functional jail complex had shrunk towards its back. As I entered there were no jail officials to take permission from. With nobody to check me, I pushed ahead. I could, however, notice some sentries standing on guard duties at the other side of the vast jail compound. They were, however, quite far away and must have taken me to be someone from the contractor's staff.

There was an isolated structure to the right looking like a jail within the jail. I entered this triangular enclosure to find myself in front of the condemned prisoners' cells—each divided in three portions, the cell, a covered verandah and an open compound. I entered some of these cells where some unfortunate beings must have spent their last days in great unease, till it was time to drag them out to the gallows in a corner of this awful triangle..

The gallows consisted of a brick-lined square pit, with a narrow staircase on one corner for the executioner to go down to deal with the dead or the dying man. On the pit was fixed a sturdy beam on two strong columns on the sides. The beam had three pulleys to deal with three convicts in one go. These brought the memories of Bhagat Singh, Raj Guru and Sukhdev, the immortal martyrs of our struggle for Independence. It gave a sunken feeling to note that these plucky freedom fighters had to die at the gallows like a common criminal.

On two sides of the pit were hinged two wooden boards. These were pulled up and joined together securely with a heavy steel bar with teeth that got pushed into the brackets on the board. These boards when up and clamped formed a platform where the condemned spent the last few minutes of their life wearing the hideous noose. The other end of the rope went over the pulley to be tied to an iron beam fixed a few yards behind the gallows. The bar on the platform was connected to a lever which when pulled by the executioner made the planks fall to the sides with a thud. Adequate play was left in the rope for the condemned fellow to fall in the pit and hang there by the neck till death.

After witnessing this awful power of the state to deal with life and death, I quietly walked out of the place without anybody bothering to take notice of me. Of course, this could be possible only because the portion of the jail visited by me then happened to be non-functional.

(A reproduction from the writer's article in 'The Tribune' of 27.6.2007.)

8

FROM MY OWN BACKYARD

Every story, told in all its intensity, is a 'Booker' candidate

93. IN THE IMAGE OF AMIR KHUSRAO

He died around forty years back. I, then a small child, stood by his burning pyre in stoic silence, firm in my belief that the pious souls like him never died. He has since lived in my mind. From this distance in time, I see him in the image of Amir Khusrao. Like the legendry laureate, he was beyond bigotry, wide-visioned, scholastic and far ahead of his age.

He had lived through the tumultuous times when the communal frenzy was at its peak. A diabolic Muslim got published a book, 'Sita–ka-Chhinala' (Rape of Sita) in Lahore. Not to be outdone in stupidity, a Hindu fanatic retaliated with 'Rangila Rasool' and paid for it with his life. Soon after, was to follow the holocaust of the Partition.

This my ancestor, Diwan Munshi Ram, was incidentally a 'munshi' by profession also. While Khusrao wrote 'masnavis' (biographies) he had to be content writing mundane petitions for his living. When he was not writing petitions for his clients, he used to be reading. The Quranic literature fascinated him the most. When I saw him so completely lost in reading, I always wondered what he was looking for. He appeared to be searching for his soul in the books.

Even at this tender age, he took me as his conscience-keeper. Whenever, something in the books touched his heart, he always had an urge to share it with me. A day before his death, I saw him doting over a voluminous book. The usual serenity and sense of bliss in his looks suddenly widened and he beckoned me to his side.

This time, it was the story of Sultan Nasir-ud-din of the Slave dynasty that ruled India in most part of the thirteenth century. The history part of it is that after the death of Altamas, his illustrious daughter Razia Begum ruled India for about four years. On her elimination, her none too worthy brothers took their turn on the throne for a while. Finally, the rulership devolved on Nasir-ud-din. The history knows him for his saintly inclinations. He appropriated no money for his domestic expenses from the state treasury and instead, made his living by writing calligraphic copies of the Quran. Quite naturally, his Begum also had to perform all the house-hold chores like fetching water from the well, cooking food and spinning on her charkha etc. It is not unusual for some mythological stories to get inter-twined with the historical facts in such situations. This particular episode recorded that Nasir-ud-din's Begum was blessed with the divine capacity to draw water from the well with just a few strands of raw cotton yarn spun by her on her charkha. In some moment of weakness, the virtuous wife felt a little impatient with her burdensome routine, and enquired of her husband why they could not draw money from the state coffers to meet their domestic needs. The saintly Sultan readily agreed that this could most certainly be done, but he explained that after that she would not be able to draw water from the well with the raw cotton thread. The reply enlightened the lady in to silence on this issue for ever.

Those were the Partition days. There was hatred for the Muslim in the air and there were bodies and blood in the streets below. Here, in his first floor apartment, sat a man grieving over the slaughter on both sides of the border and still prepared to welcome light from whatever source it came. He wrote no poetry, but his life itself was poetry of a sort. Like Khusrao, he did not seem to belong to the age in which he lived and died.

(A reproduction from the writer's article in 'The Statesman' of 3.12.1995.)

94. THE LIFE THEN

Living then seemed to be a much simpler affair—no problems about children's admission, no tension over inflated bills or some licence overdue for renewal or some gadget or the other going dysfunctional and needing repairs/replacement. In fact, the only sophisticated gadgets with the middle class families were then the bicycle and the sewing machine. Life was much less competitive and everybody seemed to have time on hand to just to 'stand and stare' without much care in the world.

While the world at the time was fighting a furious war right in our neighbourhood, we lived in near blissful ignorance at a place called 'Jaitu', an important agro-marketing centre of the princely state of Nabha in Punjab. We resided in a barrack like room, having an equally longish covered verandah in front and a big courtyard further ahead. All this was built over a big complex consisting of shops and godowns. Adjacent to our dwelling place we had a vast open terrace where a complete marriage party could be accommodated. The type of people we were this space often came very handy to us.

On one such occasion at midnight we found half a dozen sturdy 'jutts' (Sikh farmers) knocking gently at our door below the staircase. Trying to sound humble like a damsel in distress, they told us in their otherwise husky voice that they were from village Mehraj. The caretaker of the local 'sarai' (inn) had refused to let them in and they had nowhere else to go at this unearthly hour. Roaming out in the open, they feared being rounded up by the police.

The men looked weary and dog-tired. Moreover, they were from a village that had fraternal ties, running through history, with our own village, Phul. These two villages were founded by two brothers. One of them, Baba Phul, is, in fact, the founder of the Phulkian states of Patiala, Nabha and Jind. Responding warmly to their entreaties for shelter, the eldest brother of my grandfather, whom all of us fondly addressed as 'Bade Tayaji, graciously said that even a dog from the village deserved to be held in good regard and they, as honourable guests from our brotherly village, were most welcome. This was, of course, said to put them at instant ease. Otherwise, they would have been equally well treated, had they been from elsewhere.

The lady of the home, my mother, was woken up. Available cots and beddings were produced and the guests were soon made comfortable. My father and all the others also soon joined in looking after them. The sleepy eyes now wore a serene look. I, a five year old then, could also not remain unaffected by the ardour of others and found myself running errands for them. About one seer of dal and around fifty chapatti's had to be cooked for them. Pure 'desi' ghee was used for the purpose, though vegetable ghee had also then come to be used sparingly in our household.

As the food was getting ready, our guests were kept engaged in warm and lively conversation. Pointing to me, they enquired how 'Kakaji' was doing. Our Bade Tayaji replied animatedly with a glitter in his eyes that I was about to be promoted to 'Pakki' (the second term of the first standard—the first being the 'Kachchi'). The fatigued and famished men slept on their full stomach to our satisfaction.

Early in the morning, they departed but not before praying for our welfare. Their prayers seemed to come somewhere from deep inside. Finally, addressing my mother from behind the curtain on the door, they said, "Jeondi reh, Beeba". (Long live, our gentle daughter). My mother did live fairly long, but more importantly, she died in peace in the manner of a person going to sleep. It was, indeed, a different world—full of warmth, simplicity and affection.

(A reproduction from the writer's article in 'The Hindustan Times' of 4.5.1998.)

95. FADING INTO ETERNITY

His mind already seems to have wandered away from this world, but his soul is still stuck here. My father lies semi-conscious on a hospital bed at Bikaner with left side of his body paralysed. Often he takes his right hand instinctively to his head where a pool of blood has been formed due to hemorrhage. This loose blood, pressing against his brain tissues, has damaged his cognitive capacity. For all practical purposes the stroke has snatched him from us.

Some 50 years back the father-son relationship among us got pushed to the backyard of our minds and entirely new bond of friendship got gradually forged. We could now open our hearts to many new areas. At stake now are, thus, not only the filial ties but also this companionship of half a century. Yet, we are already reconciled to his loss. After all, he is 94 and all these years have been well-lived. Even minutes before the paralytic attack, he was firmly in command as head of our family— sharing our situations, shouting instructions and eager to extend his helping hand to the people in problem. This, no doubt, would never be the same for us again. But, what else can be asked from God for him? He has already lived many memorable moments in his long life and is leaving for us a bagful of memories.

Like every father, he always had exaggerated ideas about our abilities. We, the brothers, are fairly well-placed in our lives, but do not have pretensions to any sort of extra-ordinariness. Still, it feels good that there is at least one person on earth who thinks no end of us. All of us like to live with small little illusions. Even the British had illusions of permanence about their rule. Sadly, all this would be over for us as he closes his eyes on this world.

As for him, every human being has two aspects to his personality. As our father, he has been a sort of institution for us. As a person of blood and bones, he must surely be an ordinary mortal. Still, on balance, he has been a benign, well-meaning and worthy individual. We are sure, the people who came close to him in his life would not dispute this view.

We are told that there are three ways of getting to God — "Gyan Yoga" (through knowledge), "Bhakti Yoga" (through faith) and

"Karma Yoga" (by just doing one's worldly duties well). Our father was not much of a thinker. However, he was, undoubtedly, a man of faith and a great doer. We believe that his attainments in these areas would serve him well and take him safely and surely to his salvation.

If he rises from the ashes to read this, it would, indeed, be a divine miracle.

(A reproduction from the writer's article in 'The Tribune' of 2.12.2006)

96. SMILING OUT OF LIFE

Death holds two horrors. One, of course, is that life comes to an end and thus, the "fear of the unknown" factor comes in to play. Bravery and wisdom lie in coming to terms with this reality so as to die just one death. The second element is that the process of dying is also often painful.

My mother was a lady of faith and firmly believed in life after death. So, the end of one life did not mean the end of everything to her. Some 25 years back she died in the manner of a person falling asleep.

Long back, I had made a promise to her that when I grew up and settled down I would purchase a car and take her on pilgrimage to Badrinathji, one of our celebrated "dhams" located in the upper reaches of Himalayas. The promise at that point of time was like a child telling his mother that he would purchase a private jet one day to take her places. Though my mother never doubted my sincerity she felt that I was promising moon out of my innocent immaturity.

My sentiment had its seeds in the religious zeal or perhaps a streak of adventure in my grandmother. Every year or so, she would leave for places like Badrinathji, Kedarnathji and Gangotri etc in the company of some like-minded ladies and return after weeks with swellings and blisters. When we heard her stories I could see a distinct wish in my mother's eyes to be able to make to some of these places herself some day. Pilgrimage to Badrinathji always appeared to be the uppermost on her mind.

Nearly 30 years after my word to her, I was able to manage a secondhand Fiat car. Possibly, it had covered much more distance than what its milometer indicated. The surface below its engine-head had turned like a cricket pitch on the fifth day, so much so that water from the radiator would mix with the circulating engine oil. Threadings were also worn out in many of its grooves to spring surprises on me at regular intervals. But I was in a hurry to redeem my undertaking to my mother.

So, ignoring the suspect roadworthiness of my car, I left with my mother for the promised pilgrimage. Driving a worn-out Fiat over mountainous roads, especially in the unsettled Belagachi area where massive melting of a mountain face had taken a heavy toll of human lives only the other day was a real adventure. Sometimes the gear lever with worn-out threads would suddenly pop out, another time the engine oil pipeline would get detached spraying the oil over the engine block and once the drain-cock of the petrol tank was hit by a stone and whole of petrol got drained. Finally, however, we made it to the shrine.

I do not know what I prayed for at the place. Surely, however, if I were to pray for anything today I would like to smile out of life the way my mother did.

(A reproduction from the writer's article in 'The Tribune' of 12.4.2006.)

97. A SHORT JOURNEY

He was born at a time when the euphoria over our Independence had not yet worn thin. It was, indeed, a 'bliss in that dawn to be alive'. There was hope in hearts and dreams in eyes. The workers at the Bhakra Dam felt as if they were constructing their own house. In tune with the times, I suggested that he be named as 'Bharat' and this met ready approval of our family. A good fifteen years separated us. Thus, more than a brother he was a son to me. I had a sort of an illusion of immortality about him. I thought that he was going to be the permanent fixture of my life. By this, I meant the he would always be around till I was there.

Bharat grew up to be a charming young man. Though we could be easily recognized as brothers, he was a lot more handsome. As he settled down in life as a bank manager, we took care to see that he married a lady of matching charm. With a beautiful wife and two sweet kids at home and the immense popularity that he enjoyed at his place of work, life looked full of bliss for him. Then suddenly a tragedy struck. His wife's brother got into trouble at the hands of his in-laws who filed a police case against him for dowry-related cruelty. Along with him were tagged his parents, sister and her husband (my brother). Thus, the unwary young man found himself involved in a criminal case, the first in the known history of our family.

I, being the eldest son in the family and having a police and magisterial background, was naturally the first to be summoned for help in the situation. As the self-appointed mediator, I went in to a number of argument sessions with the estranged couple. The first ray of hope appeared when I discovered that they still felt some affection and concern for each other. I spoke to the concerned police officers and found them helpful. In fact, they readily agreed to work towards closing the case, if the two parties reconciled. Yet, some ego problems persisted and I had to return with the job only half done. However, the big consolation was that the anticipatory bail in the case had already been obtained for all.

The next call for me came when I was myself in excruciating physical pain. I told my brother about my inability to come, but briefed him on telephone about what still needed to be done in the case. The young man bore it gracefully appreciating my predicament. But then I could not bear leaving him to the wolves, while I was still alive. So, despite all discomfort and pain, I rushed to the place seven hundred kilometers away, putting reliance on just some painkillers. I saw my brother first. He did look a little low, but instantly brightened up when he saw me at the place. His eyes seemed to say, "Now, that is like a brother". Another round of negotiations and police formalities ensued and finally, everything fell in place and the case was happily settled.

Alas, our Bharat did not live very long after this ordeal. There is a medical theory that everybody generally suffers a mild heart-attack in his thirties which mostly goes unnoticed. Sometimes, the problem is a lot more severe. This exactly was the case with my brother. When the attack occurred, quite some valuable time was lost in persuading the young man to go in for a medical check-up. Even then he insisted on walking all the way to the intensive care unit. Thus, the young fellow was finally felled by his foolhardiness.

We are still not reconciled to his leaving us the way he did. There is just one little satisfaction that he did not die feeling lonely, since all of us kept him company till that final frontier.

(A reproduction from the writer's article in 'The Hindustan Times of 9.6.1998.)

98. 'APPAREL OFT PROCLAIMS THE MAN'

Everybody in the armed forces—be he a general or a jawan, who has not gone for a proper beard must shave in the morning. I parted company with the armed forces many years ago, but the habit refuses to leave me—once a soldier always a soldier. Every unshaven person (Late Chandra Shekhar, Chandrababu Naidu, Nitish Kumar, Narendra Modi and the like will please excuse me) looks to me to be a pick-pocket.

A beard that barely covers the chin also appears outlandish. Had I been in the position of Laloo Prasad Yadav, the then king-maker, I would have made Late I.K. Gujral's becoming the Prime Minister conditional on his doing something about his niggardly beard. I am particularly unhappy over the fact that now the noted youngsters like Sachin Tendulkar are also trying to follow in his footsteps.

I am, in fact, face to face with this problem in my own home. My son (incidentally, chander Shekhar by name) is also allergic to regular shaving. Sometimes in 1993, he landed at new York as the managing director of a travel company that had managed the tour of about one hundred and twenty delegates from this country to a conference called the 'World Vision 2000' at Chicago, the historic venue where a spiritual discourse by Swami Vivekanand had cast a magic spell on the audience hundred years back. The group consisted of a good number of V.I.P.`s who, as usual, kept him busy and worried with all sort of demands right till the very end.

As a result of this he was wearing one-and-a-half-day old beard when facing the immigration officials at the American airport. These officials are all the time weary of passengers, particularly from our part of the world, who manage to enter their country on some excuse and then play the vanishing trick on them. My son, with 'bagharh billa' (male cat) look like Nitish Kumar, did not at all match their perception of a managing director. They thought a M.D. should look a lot different—three-piece suit, bow tie, bulging chin, shaven cheeks, cigar in mouth, rolling eyes, a female secretary in tow, and much else. Here was a wiry young man in tee-shirt, growing stubs. Thus, they were very suspicious of him and summoned him to the interrogation room. After grilling him for good half an hour, they reluctantly came to the conclusion everything was right with him, expect his beard.

When I learnt about it on his return, I felt grateful to the Americans. I thought the young man, having learnt a lesson at their hands, would never be seen wearing an uncouth look in future. But I was wrong. Bad habits die hard. Recently, I found him growing stubby hair over his cheeks again. Seeing a look of strong disapproval in my eyes, he explained that he had decided to pay a visit to Mata Vaishnu Devi. Indeed, after skipping the morning shaves for about a week, he did go for the promised pilgrimage. But I wonder if his sudden interest in various 'Mata`s' is not just an excuse to avail the bliss of not having to shave every morning.

(A reproduction from the writer's article in 'The Hindustan Times' of 15.5.199

99. A NEWS FOR ME

Like many children of his age, he did not then have a care in the world and, as a five year old, he had wandered away from home for the third time. When finally located a couple of miles away from home, he did not look even half as rattled as we. Before answering any of our angry queries, he demanded to know why it took us so long to find him.

Back from his school another day, he appeared to be in highest of spirits as usual. With an elegant jerk of his upper half, he deftly got rid of his school bag at his back which was almost of half his body weight. It was now time for him to run to his mummy for a snack, but he suddenly seemed to have remembered something. He fished out a card from his bag and tossed it in front of me. And just to save me the bother of reading it, he announced, "My half-yearly result is out. Pass in four, fail in two".

Though what I heard was only the 5th standard result of my son, the 'fail in two' part of it instantly put me in a bad mood. The high hopes I had placed in the lad came crumbling down. I wondered if he had the potential to come good in anything. Often I saw him keeping wickets of the cricket team of his school. Half a dozen dives and rolls was a usual thing for him, but he was hardly able to stop a wayward ball. The bloke had the gusto and exuberance alright, he lacked in seriousness and quiet competency. He always returned from the game with his dress soiled all over and nothing else to talk about.

While I was thus lost in anxiety about his future, he stood in front of me innocently bewildered. He did not seem to know what the fuss was about. After all, he had passed in two-third of the subjects. Looking at me, however, he realized that something was badly amiss. It was perhaps necessary to pass in all the subjects and he did ensure that in the coming years; but his overall performance had nothing in it to write home about. Then suddenly he secured around 70% marks in his secondary school examination and followed it up with 83% marks in his senior secondary. Some of my earlier hopes in him came crowding back in my breast.

Now my only worry was that I had never heard a word of English from him and spoken English was the key to a career in our country.

So, now it was time to give him some exposure through the interviews and that would gradually give him some confidence to express himself in English. I made him apply for a commission in the engineering cadre of the Indian Navy and admitted in a private academy for coaching. A retired brigadier who ran the institution interviewed him. His very first question was who he loved most, Mummy or Daddy. While I waited with a look of anxiety and embarrassment in my knowledge that he would not be able to answer the question in English, my son quietly replied in chaste English that it was difficult to answer this question in the presence of the Daddy. His confidence and clarity was news for me and I was now clear in my mind that I had discovered my child. Then onward I stopped worrying for his future. He was soon off to Bangalore for his S.S.B. and on the fourth day, there was a telegram from him—-"Selected'. Then onward there was no looking back as he made it to the M.B.B.S. and the M.D. also, both in the first attempt. He has since made quite a name for himself as a senior consultant in the neonatology department of a premier hospital. In his T.V. interviews he appears to be most erudite, selecting his words with meticulous care.

I had been in the business of commanding soldiers for a long time. If a thousand men were lined up before me, I, thought, I could always tell in a moment what they were up to and how well they were likely to do in operations. How curious that it took me so long to know my own child!

(A reproduction from the writer's article in 'The Hindustan Times' of 30.9.1997.)

100. THE PEACE-MAKER

She had just been brought to her hospital bed from the labour-room, calm and sleepy. Her mind still seemed to be buckled to the world from where she had come. With two tiny roses in her dimpling cheeks, she looked incredibly cute and comely. She would blink for a while, as if to see where exactly she had landed and then recede into herself, as if wondering whether someone had done the right thing by sending her to the world again. For us, she was the loveliest gift of God bestowed upon us.

By her side lay my wife, still in some pain and discomfort, but otherwise proud to have given birth to such a pretty child. The two looked amazingly alike. I knew my wife only from the age of around fifteen. Her babyhood was a mystery to me. Now this little thing seemed to give me a glimpse into this period.

While the newborn apparently slept in peace, many expressions were passing in a procession on her face. Just when she appeared to be curling her lips to cry over something, she would suddenly change her mood and instead, pour out a smile. We had never known anything so sweet and fresh than her first smile. It was simply something out of this world. This smile decided what we were going to call her. From now onward, she was to be our, 'Lily'. To go well with this pet name, we formally named her as 'Lalita'. After her marriage, her loving husband started calling her 'Lolita'—perhaps the name 'Lalita' made his mind slip involuntarily to the grand old lady of those days, Lalita Pawar.

Anyway, our little Lily duly grew in to a beautiful girl. Around this time, we were to discover that her real beauty and worth lay elsewhere. There was something angelic about her. For one, she was a peace-maker par excellence. She seemed to have somehow acquired the skill to spot the rising surge of anger inside a person. At the first signs of the gathering storm, she would join the battle for peace, heavily armed with her familiar smile, sweet temper and a pleasing sense of humour. She would remain in huddle with the warring parties for hours, till at least one of the two surrendered. She seemed to work on the principle that everybody had a fundamental right to get angry for a while and this must be respected and accommodated.

My elder son has been one of the hardest nuts to crack. At least, in the matter of obstinacy, he has taken after me. I remember from my school days that once my school teacher was so deeply annoyed over something silly done by me that he went and brought the headmaster to deal with me. The headmaster gave me two options: either to apologize to my teacher or be ready to get severely pandied. I remember to have readily extended my hand to take the punishment, which was, of course, delivered with a vengeance.

My son once did something equally silly which made me feel awfully cut up with him. A lot of tension was thus pumped into our otherwise happy home. This was naturally the time for our family peace-maker to spring to action. She did not try at my end, simply because she knew that I had a reasonable case to feel unhappy about. However, I spotted her in huddle with my son while leaving for office. I returned in the evening still feeling tense and uneasy. Just when I settled down hoping to be served a cup of tea, something infinitely more refreshing was served to me. My son made a sudden appearance before me looking all red in the face and said, "Sorry, Daddy". Then he disappeared as quickly as he had come leaving me dazed. That was enough to dissolve all tension. For a while, I felt puzzled how the bloke could bring himself round to utter those two difficult words. Soon, however, I remembered the angel in our home. So, the 'Lily magic' had worked yet again. For a moment I thought our little lady deserved the Nobel Peace Prize.

(A reproduction from the writer's article in 'The Hindustan Times' of 23.12.1997.)

101. THE SURPLUS CHILD

When it was time to raise our family early in the last sixties, people in our social strata had just begun to bother about family planning. A proper motivation to limit the family normally emerged only after one already had three children—preferably, two sons and one daughter. The 'Hum do, hamare do' idea (which now stands refined to 'One is Fun') had not then taken root in peoples` mind. So, we also wanted to have three children before calling it a day. My numerous postings in the operational areas took care of the spacing part of it.

After we had our three children, we started practicing various sort of family planning methods which did not quite work in the end. Thus, we were going to have an unwanted fourth child. We, however, could not somehow bring ourselves round to abort it. In any case, abortion otherwise also had not been legalized by then. As it happens in such situations we promptly put what had happened on the will of God, as if He and not we, were responsible for all this. Nonetheless, both of us quietly went for sterilization operations, even without informing each other, as we had no heart to blame God any further for our next failure on the family planning front. Though it meant a little overdoing, it worked well as we did not look beyond each other. There was hardly need for either of us to keep the options open.

In due course, we had our lovely little daughter before us in flesh and blood. We could have done without her till we had seen her, but not now. One look at her pretty face just made us forget that we once did not wish to have the fourth child. Nonetheless, when our first three children got settled in their lives, a thought would occasionally cross our minds that had she not been there, we would have been free from all our primary duties by our family and thus reached the stage of our salvation right then. However, when we looked at the vivacious girl, full of life, such ideas got quickly dislodged. If even after this, we called her our 'surplus bitia', it was just to tease her for fun.

As she grew in to a highly comely, erudite and intelligent girl, we gave her in marriage to her campus mate of Delhi University, a jealously affectionate and highly possessive husband. As is the wont in our families, we called her to our place for the first delivery. We arranged for her to deliver in the LNJP Hospital in the Capital where her cousin then happened to be studying for her post-graduation in Gynaecology.

When her young husband learnt that we were going to arrange for her delivery in a government hospital, he straightaway got worried. His perception of a public hospital was that of a crowded general ward where two patients shared a single bed or were made to lie on beds made on the floor. He could not bear the thought of his beloved wife lying uncared in a corner of the general ward or sharing the dirty linen of a bed with another patient. With anxiety on this count eating him badly, he rang me up to suggest that we should move her, instead, to a good private hospital.

Even when my explaining that his wife would be there in a private ward, under the personal care of her cousin also did not satisfy him, I got a little exasperated and said, "Oh come on, son. After all, she is my child too". The tenacious young man was still very adamant and insisted that I had four children whereas he had only one wife to feel concerned about. What he said would have made better sense if I had four wives, instead of four children. Still, it was heart-warming to note that our 'surplus child' was so awfully important to him.

(A reproduction from the writer's article in 'The Hindustan Times' of 9.3.1998.)

102. THE BONDS THAT WOULD NOT SNAP

My father was the head of a government high school and got a decent salary. In fact, he was the highest paid official in the village and some simple folks there wondered what he must be doing with all the money that he got. He, however, had ten of us to feed, clothe and educate and all of us secretly shared a feeling of financial stringency.

When I graduated and got the job of an auditor in the accounts establishment of the Bhakra Nangal Project, my father felt visibly relieved. His eldest son, he thought, was now in a position to share some of his family burden with him and the others would also join in one by one in course of time. So, he could look ahead for some relief from the feelings of worry and want that always lurked around him.

Our job was to keep an eye on the accounts of a civil engineering department in Rajasthan which, even in those days, worked under an environment of institutionalized corruption. The contractors had to pay a routine cut of ten percent on passing of every bill and this amount was distributed among various functionaries according to a pre-agreed arrangement. The bills came to us for audit when everything was already over and thus, our people were left high and dry. There was some talk about introduction of a system of pre-audit of bills and many of us were hopefully looking forward to it.

I had little liking for the job. I found it mundane and monotonous. Finding fault with others somehow goes against the grain of my nature. Moreover, I thought that working at this nondescript place in such an ethos, would gradually knock all sense of ambition out of me. I felt that, with my first class degree, I should be looking for some something much better in my life than the job that I held.

So, I resigned my job to begin my career afresh in Delhi. I knew that I was taking a great risk and may have to rough it out in the capital for an indefinite period. But I was confident of coming good in the end. My father was expectedly upset over my resigning the government job without any alternative in my hand. He knew that I had the potential to do better, but by now he was a tired man, desperately in need of a helping hand. He made no secret of his exasperation and disenchantment with me. This was quite understandable in his circumstances. Yet I felt hurt and cut up over his impatience. He gave me a feeling that I had turned out to be a bad egg. I felt as if I was being abandoned. A lot had silently gone wrong between the two of us. Nonetheless, I was ready to face the wide world of my own. In fact, it was he who had prepared me for this.

Putting all this out of my system, I landed at Delhi, sure and confident of myself. Soon I found a job of a teacher to subsist and was able to purchase a secondhand bicycle and even collected a little amount in my saving bank account. The life was, of course, hard. I had to cycle my way to work to a place around twenty kilometers away. On my way back I had to cycle in the summer sun. I was eventually felled by a severe sun stroke. When, on an occasion, my temperature rose to 107 degrees, my students felt alarmed and secretly sent a telegram to my father, much against my will.

There he was by my side the very next day. During my short illness, he acted as both father and mother to me. I never knew he could be so concerned and caring. I was soon up on my feet, thanks to his loving care. As he prepared to leave, I withdrew my entire amount in my saving bank account and placed it at his disposal. He, however, refused to take it saying that at least this much amount I always needed to have with me for any possible contingency. Suddenly, the father and son had rediscovered each other.

(A reproduction from the writer's article in 'The Hindustan Times' of 21.1.2000.)

103. A GREAT BATH-ROOM SINGER

Though one can never be sure in such matters, my son, Ajay, could well be one of the loudest and most versatile bath-room singers the world has ever produced. Outside the bath-room he is perfectly normal and in fact, quite a melodious voice. But once inside, he sings with such gay abandon, as if he is all by himself in a wilderness and nobody is listening to him.

In a matter of minutes, countless songs get slaughtered at the altar of his mood. The most vulnerable are the husky compositions in Amitabh Bachchan's or Amitabh Bachchan-like voice (Mere angane mein——, for instance). However, he has the capacity to give a 'khusra-like' treatment even to the most lilting tunes. Rarely does a tune get the delicate treatment that it deserves through his vocal chords. Still he often manages to sound sweet at the start. Soon, however, the sweetness suddenly turns in to shrillness or huskiness, as he invariably loses control over the rhythm midway. He then tries his hand at his nasal talents also to provide instrumental support to his singing. When even this does not work he just skips over to the next song. Occasionally, he goes for 'alaap' also, but in no time the 'surs' start playing truant with him and he suddenly drops all this as a bad idea.

Music seems to have entered the new millennium on a rather frivolous note, but this suits his bath-room singing marvelously well. The casual and carefree compositions, often lacking in depth, are ideally suited for such cavalier treatment, as such songs can be easily crucified without any sort of burden on one's conscience. I must, however, admit that his vocal treatment roughs up even the most lilting tunes of the Sixties and Seventies of the century gone by. But I do not think Rafi, Mukesh, Talat and Kishore have to turn in their graves for this. Assault on their tunes is, of course, murderous, but there is a sort of innocence in this sonic mayhem. After all, my son is not in the bath-room for 'riyaz' by any chance, but only to contend with having to bathe. And then, everybody in our free country has the right to private singing. In fact, the "Gana aye ya na aye, gana chahiye" theory has world-wide acceptance.

Normally, there is no pattern in bath-room singing. Songs just get picked up at random according to the prevailing mood of the singer-cum-bather. However, in case of my erratic son, there is a method in his madness. Being the son of a soldier, he has a particular fondness for numbers that talk about attacks (Akhion se goli marey—), fights (Muqabla hoga—), wars (Zindagi har gharhi ek nayi jang hai—), dying (Kar chale hum fida jano-tan sathio—), blood (Khoon jigar ka doonga—) and wounds (Kis ko dikhlain zakhme dil apna—) and so on.

Nobody in our home ever had any particular objection to his singing in the bath-room. After all everybody tries his hand on singing in privacy. Nonetheless, I thought he would get cured of this noisy habit after the responsibilities of married life engulf him. But, no, after his marriage, the notes that emanate once he steps into the bath-room are even more full-throated and louder— which at least I, read as a sign of blissful contentment.

(A reproduction from the writer's article in 'The Hindustan Times' of 24.4.2000.)

104. 'CHAR BAHU-RANIYAN'

Though I did not understand then, I know very well now that my late parents did make some earnest effort to limit our family. Sadly, during their time there were no properly workable family planning devices adequately known to common people. So, they ended up having ten children, not at all an unusual phenomenon for their age.

One of us, the five brothers, went missing in a 'Kumbh mela' some fifty years back. The rest of us duly brought four 'bahu-ranis' (brides) to our house-hold—Vijay, Anjana, Usha and Sunita— in course of time. My parents remained happy and contented about them till their last breath.

So far as woman is concerned every society has blood on its hands. Over the ages, the 'bahu-ranis' in particular have suffered terribly hard. Even their parents are made to feel humble. Our Hindu scriptures require the fathers to touch the feet of the bridegrooms at the marriage ceremony. In some of our communities the mother-in-law touches the feet of her son-in-law first thing in the morning! No wonder, so many female fetuses pitifully end up in drains.

Yet, quite a few knights-in-the-shining-armour are around us now to fight for our human female—the legislatures, National Commission for Women and the Crimes against Women cells of the police (where some over-zealous officers go to the length of having the errant husbands slapped and shoe-beaten by their aggrieved wives). Still their future is generally in the nature of a lottery.

Viewed in the above context, our 'bahu-ranis' would appear to be singularly lucky. I do not recall a single instance when any of them had to suffer slightest of humiliation or hear a harsh word for being a 'bahu'. Ours has been a world where the so common 'Sas-bahu' phenomenon just seems to have missed the bus. I often wonder if this is just a happy coincidence or somebody has really worked towards it.

Our parents encouraged the 'bahus' to discard their traditional 'ghunghat' (veil) right from the Day Two, so that they might be able to move about freely as the family daughters. Their dowries were never allowed to be discussed and their blood-relations were always referred to with respect. On their part, they just mixed in our family as water in milk. I may forget about the 'shraadh' of my mother, my wife would never. None of our 'bahu-ranis' created any sort of fuss over the sizeable estate left by our parents. Rather they still dutifully fast for their well being wherever they might be now.

This, I believe, is the situation in many other families too. It is precisely for these reasons that we are the envy of the West in the matter of family life. All this, however, should not distract us from the inconvenient fact that many of our 'bahu-ranis' are still being badly treated. Much still needs to be done to improve the lot of our women, particularly the bride phase of their lives.

(A reproduction from the writer's article in 'The Tribune' of 18.4.2007.)

105. A MYSTERIOUS TRADITION

Our erstwhile British masters saw the world in only two colours—black and white. We, however, always insisted that we were neither white nor black— we were, in fact, brown. With the changing times and with Mr. Brown as the British Prime Minister, our point of view would perhaps be understood and appreciated better now.

Like most of us Indians, our family people were also always wheatish. However, wheat also comes in different colours—light as the Madhya Pradesh varieties and dark, as the Maxican strains. Now, it is quite a coincidence that in our every generation, there was one male, who though accomplished and handsome personality-wise, happened to be otherwise of a distinctly darker texture. It is yet another coincidence that these dark horses of every generation generally came good and often stole the march over the fairer ones.

Let me begin with my late great grandfather, Sh. Gurmukh Rai who was a nephew of Diwan Mahi Mal of the princely state of Nabha. He died young. So, I do not have any idea how he looked. In any case, he was an adopted child of our family. Similarly, nothing much is known about his father, Sh. Devi Dyal, his grandfather, Sh. Mollan Mal or great grandfather, Sh. Roottal Mal or great great grandfather, Sh. Jaru Mal.

True to our family tradition, my grandfather, Sh. Milkhi Ram, was of a darker complexion compared to his two elder brothers, Sh. Chhajju Ram and Sh. Munshi Ram. But he was the only one among them to get married and raise a family. Our grandmother being an exceptionally fair lady most of her children were also fair coloured. But, she also managed to keep the family tradition alive in the person of my uncle. He certainly looked quite a shade darker while standing by the side of my father, though he was conceptually more accomplished and did better than him in his career.

He was quite conscious of his colour and often confided in his 'bhavi' i.e. my mother that nobody seemed to take notice of him, though he had entered the marriage zone. 'Bhavi`s' those days were half mothers and half friends to their 'devars' and they considered it their natural duty to find brides for them. Finally, however, my uncle did not have to avail the services of my mother and was able to bring a beautiful 'aunty' to our home.

The darker lots of the next generations were my immediate younger brother and my younger son, affectionately nicknamed as 'Kalia' and 'Kalua' respectively. Both of them went on to become the pride of the family in their later life. We looked like duly living up to our family tradition when my younger grandson had to be delivered prematurely through Caesarian intervention, due to the precarious condition of our 'bahu', herself a doctor. We first prayed for her life. When she was alright we wondered, if God would be kind enough to save our child also.

Once we got the news that he had survived against all odds, our next worry was that he may be mentally deficient. My son finally conveyed that he was mentally quite alert, though he had a darker look. We heaved a sigh of relief and I wrote back: "One 'kalua' per generation was perfectly acceptable to us".

Surprisingly, our this boy, Aryan, started getting fairer as he gradually got filled up to his normal health. To add to this, he turned out to be an exceptionally smart fellow, with ability to take not only his elder brother, Rohan, but also me for a ride. We are now happy that he may not have the colour of Krishna, but he does have some of his political acumen and guile.

(A reproduction from the writer's article in 'The Tribune' of 17.12.2007.)

106. A PHILOSOPHER IN THE FAMILY

THEY were married at Lahore some 68 years back. I was around then, but too young to understand what marriage meant. My mind just took note of a lovely lady coming to stay with us seemingly from nowhere. I was to call her 'Chachiji'. My uncle, P.S. Verma, looked to be a changed person after his marriage. He seemed to emit an impression that all was well with God's world.

She was with him alive, though not exactly kicking, when my uncle entered his nineties. Sometimes back I learnt that the oldest surviving couple in the world was in the range of 96-94 years. My uncle and aunt were within the striking distance of this record, but this was not to be. This togetherness of theirs that spanned over some seven decades finally came to an end last month. The death of my aunt did them apart— only death could do it.

When I learnt about the tragedy I could feel a sense of loneliness creeping around my uncle. Earlier when we met, we went headlong in to discussion over something and vied with each other to state our views ahead of the other. Both of us had tremendous fondness for hearing our own voice. This time, however, he allowed me to monopolize all the talking. His vacant looks and stony silence sent me to a journey into our past.

Both our families lived at Lahore till tragedy of the Partition separated us. My father returned with us to the state of Nabha where one of our ancestors, a contemporary of Maharaja Ranjit Singh, once held the high position of Diwan. My uncle also managed to take the last train that could make to India safely. He got his posting at Delhi and got busy in his office routine and the education of his children.

His coaching of my cousins was not very different from the interrogation by Punjab Police. They really had tough time with him, but that saw to it that they settled down in their lives exceptionally well.

His superannuation brought him in to his own. He started delving into the philosophical aspects of the religions which happens to be my area of interest too. Thus, whenever we came together, we had animated discussions on the Vedas, the Upanishads, the Quran and the Bible etc. Last time he told me that, after fair bit of reading about the religions, he had come to the conclusion that all of these seemed to say that God was kind only to those who submit to him blindly. Otherwise He could be extremely nasty to those who raised any sort of questions. This meant that man saw God in his own image. Religions revolve around the Divine Reality alright, but otherwise these do have an unmistakable human angle to them also. How true!

(A reproduction from the writer's article in 'The Tribune' of 1.10.2008.)

107. THE END OF A STORY?

He wrote some two hundred short stories. Nearly all of these were published. A good many of these were compiled into a book and lot many went on air to the delight of the Indian expatriates in England. Yet, the most interesting story escaped his pen — the story of his own struggles.

Perhaps, writing one's own story is a real tedious task. This, in some way, involves elements of embarrassment, hesitation and also personal ego— one always feels that if one is worth a story, the others should write it. Faiz Ahmed Faiz, the celebrated Urdu poet, when once asked to pen a picture of himself, finished it in just three lines. He could not think of himself beyond being born at a particular place and time and being briefly a Colonel during World War II. It is strange that he found nothing much to write about his own eventful life, though every life if deftly described in all its emotional intensities, situational intricacies and pulsating experiences can win you the Booker's prize.

Coming back to my friend who wrote in the pen name of 'Premi', he had his roots in a wealthy family in what is now Pakistan. His parents lost their lives to their wealth and he himself, then a baby, got whisked away to the safety of Kapurthala by his mother's mother. He always had artistic inclinations and eventually his scripts and stage performances brought him considerable acclaim. The then ruler of Kapurthala and late Gobind Ballabh Pant applauded his talent. More importantly, however, his appearances on the stage won him his wife — a lovely lady from Bengal who was to stand by him through his struggles right till the very end.

In 1967, the Premi's decided to migrate to England and landed at London with just five pounds in pocket and two kids in tow. The adventurous family, however, had an over-powering urge to come good in the new land and had no desire to end up as labourers in British factories. It is said that when the going gets tough, the tough get going. Putting faith in their abilities and sweat of their brows, Mr. Premi and his wife soon moved from factories to decent white collar jobs.

They then turned their attention to the career of their kids. The years ahead continued to be a saga of struggle that saw both of their sons landing with high academic qualifications and top management positions. They may not have gone the way of Lord Swaraj Pal, Mittals and Hindujas, yet they hold a position that could be the envy of many a British.

All of a sudden, Mr. Premi died last year like a soldier with his boots on. Thus ended a manly life, full of meaning. But did it? First, I wondered whether that was all to a life. Now, I feel his story lies safely wrapped in the two hundred odd stories that he has left behind and it shall live on.

(A reproduction from the writer's article in 'The Tribune' of 28.10.2004.)

108. GRACEFUL IN GRIEF

On December 26 last, we saw the spectacle of the dreadful tsunami that descended on many Asian shores like a hungry wolf. A crisis often brings the best out of some. Thus, quite a few of the bereaved, after losing their wives and children to the waves, are known to have extended a helping hand to the marooned strangers rising above their blood. Now, how do some of us manage to stay graceful in our hour of grief?

The question took me to the backyard of my own mind where a tragedy still lies etched. Some 42 years ago, I lost my newly born son. He had appeared in this world prematurely and was, thus, too weak to take the strain of the earthly existence. Slowly, we saw his tiny limbs stiffen into death. He went as quickly as he had come.

I come from a part of the country where wailing aloud has been a tradition, if not a specialised art going by the name of "Siapa" (mourning). Just mark a line from the celebrated epic of Shah Mohammed on the Sikh wars of 1840s: — "Shah Mohammada pain ge vain doonghe, jadon hon Punjabana randian ni" (Heart rending wails will be heard all around when the Punjabi ladies lose their husbands in the war). Though I am myself not given to tears, the tragedy shattered me inside. For days I looked lost and withdrawn from the world. Then suddenly a question flashed on my mind. 'What bravery was really involved in looking bereaved?' This made me take charge of myself instantly. Perhaps the coming events were casting their shadow before.

I was soon to be a soldier and in course of time, assumed the responsibility of a Battalion Commander. The unit personnel are always like children to their commanding officers and something or the other always keeps happening in this massive family of a thousand people. I, thus, saw many of my men dying in operations and accidents. All my energies were initially bent to save my fellows. But once they were gone, I diverted my attentions to the things that could still be done for them. Rather than crying or sitting confused over their loss, I was thinking of the possibility of getting them posthumous decorations, the prompt settlement of the dues of their next of kin and keeping up the unit morale etc. All this, gave me a sense of dignity and comfort.

Recently, a dear friend of mine (incidentally working in this very newspaper) lost his mother. She was a pious lady who used to give regular commentaries on the holy Granth in a local gurdwara. She last wished to be taken to the same shrine for her final obeisance. The dutiful son carried her there and she did not live much beyond that.

My friend has a generally philosophic attitude towards life and in fact, himself a good writer. Still, however, he felt that life was never going to be the same again. I had no words to console him. So, I just narrated my own enlightening experience to him. Possibly, the light passed on to him and the same question raised its head in his mind — "What bravery is involved in appearing inconsolable?" I am sure that the stories of the tsunami braves would bring further comfort to him.

(A reproduction from the writer's article in 'The Tribune' of 14.1.2005.)

9

THE THROB OF LIFE

Life throbbing, young and quick

109. BABY's DAY OUT

Our law believes that a child below the age of seven, being incapable of planning, can commit no offence (Section 82 I.P.C.). I, however, planned the maiden adventure of life before the age of seven and made a rather meticulous job of it. The idea germinated in my mind in the Zoological Park at Lahore where our parents had taken us for an outing sometimes in1944. I was absolutely thrilled over the sight of all those animals—lions, tigers, leopards, elephants, rhinos and the rest—in flesh and blood. Earlier I had just seen their pictures in the books. I was in no way over with them, but my parents did not seem to have any more time on hand. So, I decided there and then that once was not enough and I must come back to the place again and alone.

On our way back, I took care to memorise the route. Though we had gone back in a tonga, I could guess that the zoo was around two hours walk from our house in Sant Nagar. Thus, I needed an excuse to explain my absence of around eight to nine hours—four for the round trip and four to five for roaming around in the zoo. Five hours of school time were easily available, but the problem was stretching it to nine. I soon found an answer to this. Our Sanatan Dharam School boys were soon to be taken to an exhibition laid out in the Gol Bag area, right on way to the zoo. I saw my opportunity there and decided to seize it.

The second problem was how to finance the trip. I occasionally used to be given pocket money of one paisa. Since the 'dhaila`s', (half a paisa), 'pai`s' (one third of a paisa) and 'damri`s' (one quarter of a paisa) had gone out of circulation, whole of the paisa had to be spent in one go. Overcoming my strong temptation for 'chana`s', peanuts and 'marunda' (sugar-coated baked rice) for days, I was able to accumulate a 'taka' i.e. a two paise coin for my trip. On the D-day my mother was kind enough to give me another one 'taka', along with the packed lunch, for me to enjoy my outing to the exhibition. What else could one wish for? With a fabulous amount of one 'Aana' (one sixteenth of a rupee) in my pocket and a ready excuse to be absent for eight to nine hours on top of it, I was all set for my maiden adventure.

Four hours walking was no problem for me even at that age. The only bit of a hitch to be tackled now was that the entry ticket for the zoo could deprive me of my entire cash, without which I would not be able to enjoy the occasion properly. I was, however, confident that I would be able to break through the perimeter fence. In the unlikely event of getting caught, I had only to bring myself round to instant crying at a decent pitch, which again was hardly any problem. The only hazard here was if the fellows happened to be extra kind, they might insist on delivering me to my parents. Anyway, I calculated that this much risk was well worth taking.

I duly reported to my school with the conspiratorial ideas safely tucked within. We were then taken to the exhibition site. I hurriedly went around the exhibition to be able to stand up to any possible cross-examination by my parents at the end of the day and then quietly slipped away from the place. I was soon passing by the Anarkali bazaar and some distance away to my left was the river Ravi. I thought that some other day I would similarly make it to the bank of Ravi also (and 'awaara' as I was by nature, I did).

Crashing through the zoo fence proved to be an unexpectedly smooth affair. I spent some gala time with the zoo animals. The packed lunch and the 'Aana' with me made my time even more enjoyable. I walked back home happy and contented. To my amusement, my mother felt that I must be feeling very tired after walking my way to the exhibition site and back. So, she took special care of me in the evening. She had no idea that I had already come of age that day. In fact, she continued to care for me as a child even when I was eventually commanding a battalion!

(A reproduction from the writer's article in 'The Hindustan Times' of 7.8.1998.)

110. THE CHANGING CONTOURS

I had developed somewhat curly hair naturally, as I grew into my teens. My father, however, was unprepared to believe that it was a natural growth. He thought that I had managed the curls by pressing and pulling my hair with the back of my comb and was getting too much of a 'shokeen' (fashionable) for his comfort. So, he decided to take the things in his own hands to put an end to my churlishness. One day he was ready with a comb in hand to take on me, as I came out of the bathroom.

He made me sit in front of him and started running the comb into my hair. These were then wet, soft and yielding. He was thus able to have his way with these for a while. He parted these in the middle and pasted these on the sides neatly to give me, what he thought, was a 'beeba' (gentle) boy look. I, however, felt depressed to find myself having the appearance of a sophisticated dancing girl like 'Umrao Jan'.

Mercifully, as the hair dried up, these started curling like the suddenly broken strings of a sitar to the great exasperation of my father. All the good work done by him came to a naught. He soon left me as a bad job and never bothered me again for my hair.

After some sixty-five years my story repeated itself on my little grandson, Aryan. Just a few days back, we had a function in our family— the golden jubilee celebration of our own marriage, in fact. All our close relations had congregated at Gurgaon and were getting ready to go to a banquet hall. The gathering included another grandson of ours from London, Karan. He is a strapping young man on whom anything would look nice. In keeping with the times, he had done up his hair by lifting the jelly-applied tufts like the pyramids of Egypt. He saw young Aryan around and took him away to dress up his hair in all fondness. Aryan emerged from the room in real high spirits with his hair lifted from the sides in to a crocodile type of hump on the top. However, just as he was about to leave for the ceremony, his Naniji (mother's mother) accosted him with the words, 'Be tu ne abhi baal bhi nahi banay' (O You, you have not yet even combed your hair)? She got hold of him and combed his hair tidily to the sides.

The generous amount of jelly ensured that these stayed there. Aryan now appeared to be having no hair on the head. It just seemed to have been painted shiny black. The poor little fellow looked visibly bewildered and appeared asking what he had done to deserve this.

(A reproduction from the writer's article in 'The Tribune' of 28.3.2011.)

111. OUR BUDDING INNOVATORS

We, the people of India, could perhaps consider ourselves as the privileged people of God. We are sitting on a most hospitable piece of earth, having high fertility, abundant natural resources, temperate climate, large continental-shelves extending hundreds of miles into the seas on both sides. Besides, our shores command sea routes in all directions. Above this all, we are also blessed with high I.Q. (intelligence quotient). Our ancestry has delved deep into the mysteries of the universe and life, generating a wealth of genuine philosophy. If despite all this, we suffered slavery of a thousand years, we have to find an answer for this in our fissiparous propensity or the fact that the order of nature is just cyclic— i.e. what goes up has to come down one day in its due turn.

Today, India seems reviving and riding high on young shoulders. After all, the persons of Indian origin are the most prosperous segment of the American society on the strength of their intellectual prowess. Our innovators are gradually making their presence felt all over the world, particularly in the area of information technology.

I, as a small child, was a sort of bug-bitten kid in the matter of curiosity. Somebody had gifted me a flute. After fiddling with it for a while, I had an urge to know what produced the tunes from inside it. So, I broke it open and suffered rebuke for it. My grandson, Rohan, a 9th standard student of a Delhi Public School at Gurgaon, has similar propensities.

A few years back, Rohan, learnt about the oil spills in the oceans. He saw the spectacle of some marine birds emerging from the coastal waters, bathed in brownish oil. Ever since then, he had been working on a device to suck the oil sleek from the surface of water efficiently and economically. Thus, when his school thought of participating in an inter-school science and technology competition in the North zone, he was able to display his contraption and get selected to represent the school, along with his school-mate, Abhimanyu.

His parents were quite happy about his participation. Just when he was leaving for the venue, they found him carrying a bottle of mustard oil along. The mother jokingly reminded him that the mustard oil was quite expensive. It must not go waste and he must bring something back in lieu.

Some one hundred and sixty institutions participated in the competition and eventually, forty five of them were short-listed. When it was his turn to display his device, he spilled the mustard oil on water in a tub. He and Abhimanyu, then neatly sucked the sleek of oil from the surface with their contraption to the cheer of the crowd and the judges. The expensive oil was back in the bottle and the judges put the champion's trophy in their hands for this wonderful innovation.

It was, of course, a baby step and they have many levels yet to rise to, but a hint of promise is unmistakably there. They or the likes of them, would one day be certainly clearing the oceans of the oily sleeks at a fraction of the cost incurred and the time taken now.

(A reproduction from the writer's article in 'The Daily Post' of 31.7.2013.)

❑❑❑